PRAISE
CONSCIOUS TRANSITIONS

Andrea's words convey a deep honoring of the lives of our animal friends. This poignant book offers heart-felt guidance for everyone who is struggling or has struggled with a pet's departure. Andrea explores both the practical concerns we may have with pets who are ill and also the greater soul journeys of our beloved companions. Her graceful insights shine with sparkling wisdom on every page. And Andrea's tender honesty provides comfort for the grieving heart.

—JoLee Wingerson, *Spirit Whispering*

In *Conscious Transitions*, Andrea Floyd reminds us that we can talk to our pets and help them transition more easily.

—Anne Salisbury, PhD, MBA, author of *Eureka! Understanding and Using the Power of Your Intuition*

I have just finished reading *Conscious Transitions*. I literally cried 10 different times. Yes, tears of sorrow as I understood the feelings of loss, but also tears of recognition that Andrea so clearly could articulate how connected we are. Andrea has written a book not just about animal communication, it is also a beautiful story of love. The reawakening of the truth that we are all connected beings. You could read this book a hundred different ways, but if you have ever loved (whether it was an animal or human), I recommend you read it as a beautifully crafted handbook to understanding the soul connections we have to all our loved ones, and if you are brave like Roxy was, see it as a workbook for how you can deeply love and be loved.

"There is no final," she told me, "only the next lesson, the next remembering, the next opportunity to live in love with all around you."

—Shoshanna French
Intuitive and Coach at Simple Spirit

CONSCIOUS TRANSITIONS

Andrea L Lloyd

CONSCIOUS TRANSITIONS

Finding Comfort, Connection and Peace
When Your Pet is Dying

Andrea L. Floyd

Roxy Tales Publications

Conscious Transitions: Finding Comfort, Connection and Peace
When Your Pet Is Dying
by Andrea L. Floyd

Copyright © 2012 Andrea L. Floyd

Published by
Roxy Tales Publications / Colorado

Visit www.AndreaLFloyd.com for more information.

ISBN: 978-0-9894532-0-2

Library of Congress Control Number: 2013910603

Editing:
Cover and Interior Design: Nick Zelinger, www.nzgraphics.com
Editor: Melanie Mulhall, www.DragonheartWritingandEditing.com

First Edition

Printed in the United States

For Roxy, always.
And for Arden and EddieMac who taught me
the beauty of a conscious transition.

TABLE OF CONTENTS

ACKNOWLEDGMENTS

My husband, Jordan, is a rare and wonderful man. He understands who I am and who I am not, and loves me for all of it. His love and support are behind every word I've written.

Thank you for believing in me and giving me the courage to believe in this book.

Alicia and Liz are two wonderful women who do friendship the way dogs do love. Both of these women read the book as I was writing it and offered constructive and sometimes difficult feedback. They are also the best cheerleaders anyone could have. Thank you for giving your time to this book and to me. Thank you for reminding me to stay positive and keep going when I wanted to give up.

Joyce Leake is my animal communication mentor and inspiration. She helped me germinate the seed of this book and showed me how to tend it as it grew. Thank you for the inspiration and coaching you gave me and for your unwavering stand as an advocate for the souls in all forms.

Melanie of Dragonheart Writing and Editing has a remarkable ability to see the vision behind the writing. Add that gift to her gentle but firm handling of my "sacred cows" that needed to go and you have the perfect editor for a first time author. Thank you for making my book shine and keeping my vision intact when I lost my way.

There have been many amazing animals in my life and I have learned so much from all of them. Thank you for agreeing to come here and be my teachers. I am humbled by your devotion.

INTRODUCTION

He looks at you with soft brown eyes and you can feel his unfathomable love bathing you and seeping into your soul. You have held him and cuddled him through the years. You have comforted him and have been comforted by him. He has filled your life with joy and laughter and you have given him your love and care in return, always feeling you have gotten the better end of the bargain. He has looked at you like this many times, telling you with his eyes that he depends on you and he trusts you, always. But you have never been through *this* with him before. You have never had to deal with the ending of his body, his impending death, and you do not know how you can possibly face the choices you must make and the empty spot his passing will create.

For those who have had this experience, the pain may even have been made worse by having to make the choice to end his life, to ease his suffering through euthanasia. If you have had to make this choice, you are probably familiar with the guilt it can cause, even when it feels right. You may have felt the anguish of wondering if you did the right thing, and you may have wondered if your animal companion was scared or confused by what you were doing. If so, you have carried the burden of making a choice and taking an action that ended the life of the animal you loved, the animal who trusted you to take care of him.

Sometimes our animals leave their bodies on their own, without warning or after a long illness, maybe even when we aren't there. Then we wonder what more we could have done. Did we fail our animal companions and let them suffer needlessly? Did they die wondering where we were and feeling abandoned?

I dare say, many of us who have lost animal friends to illness or old age have longed to talk with them about their illness and their impending death and know for certain that we were taking the steps our animals wanted. We've yearned to hear from them how they felt, emotionally and physically, what they wanted and needed from us as they approached the ending of this life.

For some of us, this thought of communicating with our animals is more than a passing fantasy. It is a reality and a way of life. I have had the honor, privilege, and pain of helping several of my animal companions transition from life to life, and I am so thankful that I learned how to talk with them about what was happening. Our animals are spiritual beings. They have souls and life plans just as we do. And they are eager to share their experiences with us, to learn and grow with us, especially around their time of transition.

I am no more gifted than you are. It is within you to reach out and communicate with your dear animal companions.* This guide and workbook are designed to aid you in helping your animal to achieve a conscious transition, one in which both of you are not only fully present to each moment, but also aware of what is wanted and needed, and more importantly, aware of how much you mean to each other.

*There is real science behind the art of interspecies communication! If you would like to learn more about this innate ability we all share I recommend reading *Decoding the Mystery of Interspecies Communication* by Joyce Leake and Vickie Wickhorst, PhD.

CHAPTER ONE

What is a Conscious Transition?

Arden

It's early spring in Colorado, a soft evening that hums with the promise of budding leaves and tiny green shoots soon to come. I'm sitting on a couch in our den, holding Arden, our fourteen-year-old cocker spaniel girl. I'm surprised that she left the office upstairs and her special person, my husband, to come and sit with me. But when she starts to talk with me, to make her request of me, my only thought is, "No, please not so soon!"

She is still a vivacious puppy girl in my eyes, running with abandon and barking for sheer joy at butterflies. But it is her shining soul surrounding her body that I see, and not her body itself. Her once steady and sure gait is now wobbly. She's missing one of her beautiful brown eyes, a casualty to glaucoma. And there's a bare, rough patch of skin just in front of her tail, skin permanently damaged from radiation treatments. Arden has been battling mast cell cancer for over a year now, and she has come to tell me the fight is over.

Arden snuggles up to my side and then I hear her voice in my mind.

"Mom, I'm tired. I don't want any more chemo or radiation; I don't want any more surgeries. I have things to do. I want to go. Please say it's okay. And please help Dad. He's never lost anyone before and he doesn't know how. I trust you to do what I need. Let me be free of this body."

In the stillness of that moment, with Arden's request hanging heavy in the space between us, I think of our life together. I think of all the times I have spoken with love and pride of my Arden. She belongs to me and I . . . I belong to her. I hug Arden to me while my tears begin to flow. We belong to each other and I tell her, "Yes, I will help you."

Conscious:
To be present and aware.

Transition:
To change or move from point A to point B or from one state of being to another.

What does it mean to be conscious? On its most basic level it means to be aware and functional in your environment. But there is a whole world of consciousness beyond that. The word "conscious" represents a powerful concept. To be fully conscious is to be aware and present in each moment. It means having your mental faculties fully active! When you are fully conscious you will be aware of and sensitive to the world around you and the relationships you participate in.

You will have all of your senses and your heart, mind, and soul engaged and active. You will see the beautiful sunset, even in rush hour traffic, and you will truly hear the communications of others. You will be aware of your world and able to choose how you interact with others.

What does it mean to transition? To transition is to move from point A to point B, physically or mentally. It could be a person moving from one city to the next or from high school to college. A transition of state could be water transitioning from liquid to ice or steam. In the case of water, it's still water, but as it transitions from state to state it will look and feel very different! In the case of the person, they will maintain their "personhood," but the transition will change their experience and probably how they think and feel, at least a bit.

When I talk of a conscious transition, I am referring to being present, having your mental and spiritual faculties fully active during another soul's transition of state from this life to the next. The transition begins when you first know that your animal companion will be leaving his or her body in a definable span of time. It could be hours or days. Or, as with Arden's transition, it could take over a year. No matter how long you and your animal companion have, rest assured that it will be enough time.

When you and your animal companion are creating a *conscious* transition, you are each aware of your emotions and you each allow them space to be without judgment. You ask for each other's communications and you listen with your heart and soul, as well as your ears. You take time to celebrate your life together, letting each other know what you mean to one another. You may even plan together how you will relate to one another after the transition.

Just as you need air to breathe, you need communication for a conscious transition, communication generously given and generously received. We souls in human bodies tend to have a harder time discussing death in any but the most generic of terms, but this is not so for our animal companions. We wonder and question what's next while they truly see death as a transition, a change of state in which their essence, like the water, never really changes.

You are certainly capable of communicating with your animal companion during this process, and even if you don't think you are communicating, you will be. But if you have questions or you are just learning to use your innate animal communication ability, you may want to contact a professional animal communicator. An animal communicator can help you find clarity during this emotional time and can even guide you in finding your own communication channel with your animal companion.

Shortly after Arden asked me to let her go, and only a few days away from the appointment to free her from her failing body, I saw her eyeing the peanut butter and jelly sandwich in my husband's hand. When he didn't immediately stop and give her the sandwich, she stamped her front legs emphatically and barked at him. We both clearly "heard" her say, "Hey! Short timer here. Give me the food!" Arden got the sandwich, and we had a much needed moment to laugh and cherish the indomitable spirit of our little girl.

There is beauty and grace in a conscious transition; there can be laughter to temper the tears. Give yourself room to experience all of your emotions. When you face the transition of your animal companion honestly and openly, you will find very few places to hide from what is happening. Don't let this deter you. Yes, there will be gut-wrenching moments and bittersweet days, but there will also be moments of amazing connection between you and your animal companion as you learn and grow together. And there will be laughter and joy as well. Our animal companions live very much in the *now*. They see no reason not to take a moment of fun or love—or even a bite of forbidden food—just because their journey in their current body is drawing to a close.

Chapter One Workbook Exercise

- If you and your animal companion are facing a transition right now, make a list of what you would like to say to him or her. Make a second list of the questions you would like to ask your companion.

CHAPTER TWO

Basics of Animal Communication

Andrea

At first, I didn't think I was making progress, but then something amazing and humorous happened. I was in the kennel, putting the boarders to bed for the night, when I saw one dog curled up content-edly on his new bed, muddy paws tucked beneath him on the now dirty fleece. I looked at him in exasperation and thought, "Why can't you just keep your paws off of that nice bed?"

And then I heard him, clearly, in my head.

"You put your feet on your bed don't you?"

The feel of that sentence, the smug sense of ending the discussion, were distinctly different from the resonance of my own thoughts. I had connected. I had sent and I had received. And I was amazed.

Roxy (Cocker Spaniel)

I felt your amazement, your joy at this simple communication. And in a way, I was amazed too. To me this communication was so easy, so simple. Just allow it to be and it will be effortless. But the human condition makes the simple things difficult. Reach out, touch, and immerse yourself in the continual hum of all living things. The streams of communication flow all around us, waiting only for us to wade in and allow what is to be.

Communication
To exchange ideas and concepts with another being through verbal, visual, or telepathic means.

To understand and be understood.

It seems like communicating with animals should be complex and mysterious, but really it is a very simple thing. You probably already communicate with your animal companion and are not aware of it. I have a dear friend who told me that she couldn't talk with her dog. It was beyond her. And then, not two minutes later, she told me how she hardly had to train her dog to do anything because her dog just always seemed to do what she wanted without being told. I couldn't help but laugh. Whether she recognized it or not, it was apparent that she was very much in communication with her doggie friend.

When I was a very young child, my family had a huge German Shepherd Dog named Rex. He was my best friend. I would talk with Rex for hours, pouring out my childhood concerns and dreams, and listening to the comfort he gave in return. I read my favorite books to him and found him to be a very attentive listener. As a child, I never doubted that Rex and I carried on long conversations.

I can't remember the exact moment it happened, but at some point, my parents stopped telling me that talking with Rex was sweet. Instead, they began telling me that thinking Rex and I were having a conversation was just my childish imagination. This idea was reinforced by other adults and my peers when I went to school. It was cute for a young child to talk with animals, but it was clear to me that everyone around me expected me to grow out of such fanciful notions as I matured. By late elementary school, I no longer told people about my conversations with Rex. By Jr. High, I no longer talked with Rex or believed that I could.

Years later, when I was struggling to reawaken my animal communication ability, I thought of Rex. I believe that he never stopped talking with me, never stopped telling me he loved me. And I believe he never stopped waiting for me to remember our connection.

We are all born knowing how to communicate with animals. Some of us are lucky enough never to forget our ability, but most of us forget what we know and what we can do. In part, we forget because there are so many other things to learn and experience and in part, we forget because our society expects us to. For many years, society seemed to value logic and "being realistic" over less measurable concepts like a sixth sense and the ability to talk with animals. Now, we live in an age of change, an age in which we are learning that many more things exist than we might have imagined, whether or not they can be measured or examined. The further our science progresses, the more we learn that ideas once considered paranormal are actually just normal.

In its most basic form, animal communication is simply the interaction between your electrical field and that of your animal companion. Messages are sent back and forth across the energy fields like voices from your cell phone to the cell tower and on to your friend's cell phone. In fact, if you give it some thought, it may be easier to believe that you can talk to the dog or cat sitting beside you than believe that your voice is broken down into a digital signal, beamed across the city or country, reconstituted back into your voice, and then easily heard by your friend, all in a few seconds time!

We have no trouble believing a cell phone can work because most of us use one daily. We probably rarely, if ever, stop to think of the principles that allow the cell phone to work. We just hit "send" and talk. Once you've reawakened that which is already in you and strengthened your animal communication muscle, it will be like the cell phone. You will mentally press "send" and talk, and you will rarely, if ever, stop to think of the principles that allow this communication to work.

There are many wonderful books available to guide you through the learning phase. You can also find workshops and classes to aid you. I recommend reading *Decoding the Mystery of Interspecies Communication* by Joyce Leake and Vickie Wickhorst PhD. This book will not only give you a solid foundation to rediscover your ability, but it will also give you a foundation in the science and universal laws that make this communication possible.

There are a few steps you can take right now to kick-start your natural animal communication ability:

1. Tell your socially conditioned disbelief in animal communication to take a permanent vacation. We humans once believed that Earth was the center of the universe and was flat, but that didn't stop Earth from being round and orbiting the sun.

2. Take time to meditate. Allow your mind to wander and your senses, including that inner sense of intuition, to come alive to the world around you.

3. Observe your animal companions. Take note of how they communicate with you. If you have more than one animal companion, also note how they communicate with each other.

4. Talk out loud with your animal companions. And then answer out loud for them with the first thing that comes to your mind. It may be awkward at first, but soon you will recognize the feel of their voice when they communicate with you.

We each learn at our own pace. Likewise, we each reclaim our natural animal communication at our own pace. It took me months before I had that first simple communication with the muddy dog in the boarding kennel. And it was many more months before I could finally reach out to the soul of my dear Rex. When I first started dating my husband-to-be, Jordan, I told him about my journey in animal communication. He was fascinated and asked how he could learn to talk with my dogs as well. Within a few weeks, he was carrying on lengthy conversations with all three of my dogs!

Whether your ability reemerges quickly or slowly, you will soon be talking with your animals if you persist.

Chapter Two Workbook Exercises

1. Consider your opinions on animal communication and the opinions of those around you. Journal on how those opinions have influenced your relationships with your furry friends.

2. Keep a log of the results from your experiments in talking out loud with your animals. Notice how your animals' views of the world are similar and different from yours.

CHAPTER THREE

The Promise

Roxy

Humans and animals make a promise to one another the first moment they fall in love.

"One day you must let me go," the animal says, "maybe even at your hand. You, as the human, must promise to carry out the decision to end my life when the time comes. I, as the animal, must trust you to hear me when the time comes and let me go, even if it causes tears and sorrow to flood through your soul."

It is a solemn, excruciating, reverent promise.

Capo (pronounced key-po)

It's a chilly November night with a hint of snow in the sharp air and the beginnings of frost on the brittle grass. My husband and I are bundled against the cold but our emotions are as bright and joyous as a riot of summer blooms. We are bringing home our new little puppy girl, Capo. We have waited as patiently as we could during the eight weeks she grew in her mother's belly, and the twelve weeks she stayed with her mom and two littermates while she learned how to be a dog and how to be ready to go off on her own to become our baby. She has been ours from the first day of her life, when we dropped everything and drove an hour to see the new little lives. My husband, Jordan, picked up each of the three tiny blind and deaf puppies, held them close, and marveled at their delicate perfection. He held the first-born girl the longest, feeling her soft breath on his cheek as she squirmed closer into the warmth of his skin. "This one," he said. "This one is our little girl."

Now, at last, the wait is over and we have claimed our Capo, the newest member of our family. Once we have her inside our house, we give her time to explore her new home and meet our two older dogs. Our fourteen-year-old girl, Arden, sniffs her and gives Capo her approval. I am glad for this. Arden played a role in choosing the soul we named Capo to bring into our family. She knows that in a few months she will leave her body and we will need a beguiling and spirited puppy to remind us how to laugh, play, and love without denial or reservation. Capo is entranced by Arden, sniffing her over carefully, and following her at a respectful distance.

Cruz, our nine-year-old boy, eyes Capo with suspicion. He is her canine father, and though we told him we were bringing his daughter home today, we failed to tell him what a daughter is. He is less than pleased with her attempts to tug on his ears. He finally curls up on his cushion with a long sigh and covers his ears with his paws.

When Capo has settled a bit, grown tired from exploring and playing, Jordan and I cuddle with her on our couch. We pet her long, soft ears and kiss her little black nose, laughing when she rolls over and offers us a velvety puppy belly to rub. I hug her warm and sturdy body, smelling the remnants of puppy breath as she licks my face. Without thought I give my heart to her. She meets my eyes with her own, so young and so wise at the same time. In the space of a moment I know she is giving me her heart as well, and she is asking me to take care of her always, no matter what it might cost me, because in this life where she is the dog and I am the human, all she has is trust in my promises.

I look at this beautiful little life in my arms and I give her my promise. I can do nothing else. I will always take care of her, no matter the cost, no matter how much I will one day yearn to keep her with me far longer than she wants to stay. As I look at this adorable, exuberant puppy, I know that I am holding unconditional love and loyalty,

*laughter and joy. And I am also holding heartache
and grief. I gather Capo closer to me and lay my
cheek against hers. My sudden tears morph into
laughter when she licks my nose, barks one sharp
puppy bark, and squirms out of my grasp to jump
onto Jordan's shoulder. It is a good bargain I have
made with her.*

Promise
To commit to an action or lack of action, to give
your word to another about what you will or
will not do.

What does it mean to make a promise? To make a
promise to another being, or even to yourself, is
to give your word that you will do or not do something,
be or not be something. Some promises can be made
with little thought; others may require you to search
your heart and soul. Keeping a promise requires integrity,
whether or not the promise is easy or difficult to keep.
Integrity is not a possession, but a way of being, a
choice. No matter how hard a promise may be to keep,
keeping that promise starts with *choosing* to keep it.
Even if you can't see a way to keep your promise, simply
choosing to do so will give room for your promise to be
fulfilled.

What does it mean to accept a promise? Accepting
a promise requires a step of faith. There may be actions

34

you can take to help another keep their promise to you, but at the heart of it, you are having faith in both the other being and the universe that the promise made to you will be kept.

Our lives with our animal companions are filled with promises. They promise to behave in ways that we desire (as much as possible). We promise not to ask too much of them and to remember their favorite treats. They promise to put up with ideas and actions that make no sense to them. We promise to play with them and meet their needs. These are the easy promises. There are other promises we make, human to animal and animal to human, that are far more difficult—both to make and to accept.

At the heart of all existence lies choice. Even when we feel that we have no choice, we do. We are where we are by choice. Souls not only choose to come into this life, they choose the forms they arrive in. Humans have chosen the human form and animals have chosen the animal form. All choices have benefits and opportunities—opportunities for lessons to be learned, for growth on the soul level, and for things once known and forgotten to be remembered.

To choose to be a domesticated animal is to choose to put your well-being and happiness almost entirely into the hands of another. Our dogs and cats, our birds and hamsters, our horses and pigs and cows and chickens all live their lives in a state of dependence we humans usually only experience as children. We humans asked the animals to do this, and they agreed. Each of us made a choice and we made pacts with one another. Our responsibility to our animal companions is not negated by these acts of choice but, rather, made more solemn.

When we bring animals into our lives, we are claiming this responsibility. We are promising to take care of them, look after them, and meet their physical and emotional needs. In return, the animals promise to trust us, teach us lessons that only animals can teach humans, and give us something only they can give us—genuine unconditional love.

There are many steps we can take when our animals are not behaving in the manner we ask them to, but our animal companions have little recourse but to trust that we will honor our end of the relationship.

We, animals and humans, are brought together by choice and held together by love. Every promise we keep to our animal companions we keep out of love, even the hardest promise of all.

We humans cling to this life with a fierce tenacity, often having little if any connection to the lives that have come before or will come after. Our animal companions cling to this life too, because every life holds a beautiful pull for each soul. But our animal companions are usually more connected to what has been and what will be. They are more aware of their soul as separate from the body that houses it. They are more aware that all of our relationships with and to each other, our interconnectedness, live in the eternal now. They do not choose to stay in a body racked with pain and limitation, they choose to move into a state of spirit, a state of energy, so they can continue their journey. And they ask us, they trust us, to help them.

When we bring an animal into our lives, when we fall in love with them and promise to take care of them, we are promising to let them go when they ask us to. We are promising to perform the ultimate act of love for an animal: we are promising to release them from their body, when and if the time comes, no matter how much it may hurt us to do so. We are promising to understand when the time comes and give their soul freedom, whether we must take the action we call euthanasia or we must sit quietly with them and provide space for a natural transition. Our animal companions trust us to fulfill this promise, a promise requested by one soul and granted by another.

There is another part to this promise between our animal companions and us, the promise our animals make to us. It is an easier promise to make and to fulfill and a far harder promise to trust. Our animal companions promise us that when we say good-bye to their bodies, their physicality, that we are not saying good-bye to them! Everything that is them, that animates their physical form, continues. In a universe where all energies, all beings, are connected, we can never truly be apart from another, no matter what state or form their soul chooses. It is simply a matter of knowing where and how to look for them.

Jordan and I helped our precious Arden transition from her ruined body on a warm spring morning at the Colorado State University Veterinary Teaching Hospital. We took her there for the procedure so she could say good-bye to the wonderful doctors, nurses, and volunteers who had treated her over the last year and four months and so she could leave her body surrounded by beauty and love. I have never before seen a soul so sure, so confident, and so eager to transition. Arden asked us repeatedly not to back out as we made the two-hour drive to CSU, not to be fooled by the one good day she was having, not to be tempted to ask for more than she could give.

Several of the CSU staff sat outside with us in the shade of an old and solid tree, its branches providing a secluded and blessed spot for Arden to transition. Arden took her time, going from lap to lap in the circle of people around her, saying thank you, saying I love you, saying you have been special to me. When she was ready, she walked to the center of the circle, sat down, and awaited the injection that would release her from her body.

I have always been able to feel the passing of my animals, feel when their souls take flight from their bodies. I could not feel Arden's passing. I was stunned.

After several seconds I caught Jordan's eye. "I can't feel her, I can't connect with her! Can you?"

He shook his head and just as he started to speak, we were both overwhelmed by Arden's spirit. She rushed over us like a gust of wind and I heard her shouting and laughing in my head. "*Look* at me! Look what I can do! I can be everywhere at one time!"

One moment she was gone, no longer perceptible in any way, and the next she was back, a joyful child on a cosmic skateboard showing us all the marvelous tricks she could suddenly do again. Jordan and I laughed through tears at the joy and delight her soul was sharing with us.

Even as I reconnected with Arden's soul, my thoughts were with Capo. "Yes, my darling little girl," I told her, mind to mind. "You can trust in my promise, and I can trust in yours."

Chapter Three Workbook Exercises

1. What do your animal companions trust you to do? What do you trust them to do?

2. Take a moment to think of what circumstances brought you and your animals together. What role did choice play in it?

3. Think back to the first moment you fell in love with your animal companion. Can you remember making the promise to your animal friend? If not, can you see it now? Journal on that moment, what it meant then and what it means now.

CHAPTER FOUR

The Beginning of the . . . Beginning

Andrea

I can still see the color of the late afternoon sky, the hue of the light as it washed over us. You were sitting in my lap, and I leaned down to kiss your beautiful vanilla face in that perfect spot between your eyes. I felt it then, that small, almost innocent, bump beneath your skin.

Roxy

I wanted to stay with you in the physical world, but my body was growing tired. Every day it seemed harder to hold my soul in the confines of my physical. There were more good days ahead but this was the time to prepare.

I thought, 'I must make her understand now, just in part, and the truth will be familiar when the time comes for us to carry it out.'

Beginning
The moment when something begins and/or the physical place where something begins.

Beginning is such a simple word. It represents one of the core concepts in our human view of the universe. You can begin a physical journey, a spiritual journey, or both. You can see the beginning of the path you may take. You can feel the beginning of love or the moment you begin to feel fear. We measure our lives by talking about events that happened "before" or "after." We refer to a time before our marriage or after our children were born. We speak of our lives before college or after our first job. In between each of our before and after moments is a beginning—the beginning of a transition.

Is it possible to have a beginning without an ending? We talk of the cycle of life and we mean that one thing must end for another to begin. The rabbit must end for the coyote to begin eating; the blade of grass must end for the rabbit to begin eating. But what exactly has come to an ending in these scenarios? The soul of the rabbit transitions and the body of the rabbit transitions too! Even the grass has an energetic pattern as well as a physical pattern that transition from state to state.

If there are no endings, only transitions, can we actually have a beginning? Maybe not. We use the words "beginning" and "ending" to define things before and after they transition.

Our animal companions live much more in the "now," in a world less defined by time. Even so, they are aware of our need to delineate our lives and our experiences with time, with beginnings and endings. And if they can, your animal companion will give you time to accept their coming transition. They will give you a beginning to the phase of your life with them in which you help them transition into a new state, a new beginning.

I can remember clearly all of the "beginnings of the beginnings" I have had with my animal companions, even the ones I experienced before I remembered how to communicate with my animals. In each case, there was a moment in which I knew without doubt that their transition had begun, even if I only recognized the moment on the soul level.

Your animal companion may start sleeping on the bed with you when they haven't before, or stop sleeping on the bed. You may notice that their gate has changed or there is a lump, small or large, where there wasn't one before. They may become clingy or they may seek solitude. Whatever signal they send, they are giving you time to prepare.

This is the time to talk with your animal companion and find out how he or she wants the transition to proceed.

Arden was twelve when I saw a slight thickening in the skin on her back, just in front of her tail. That was our beginning. For three days while we waited for the veterinary appointment, I told myself this thickening was part of the aging process. But just as I had known with Roxy, I knew that Arden was transitioning. The veterinarian's diagnosis confirmed my subconscious fears: Arden had mast cell cancer.

I made an appointment with the Colorado State University Veterinary Teaching Hospital's oncology department that same day. The team of CSU doctors checked her over thoroughly and gave us a guarded but hopeful prognosis. With surgery and radiation treatments, Arden might go into remission. At the very least, she would have more time with us, and possibly quality time at that. In the months my husband-to-be, Jordan, and I had been dating, he had developed a strong bond with Arden. He loved her and had found his special dog in her, just as she had found her special person in him. I couldn't make a choice without both his and Arden's input. Though Jordan had only just begun to remember his animal communication abilities, Arden chose to deliver her very clear message to him.

"I went outside with her," he told me, "and I just sat with her for a bit. I wasn't sure what to do at first. I wanted to ask her about this, I wanted to know what she wanted, but I wasn't sure if I could actually talk with a dog about something this important. I tried being quiet and 'thinking' at her, but I was getting nothing back. Finally, feeling a little silly, I started talking out loud to her. 'Arden, they say you have cancer and you need surgery if you're going to hang around here much longer. Do you want surgery or not?' And then wow! She was yelling in my head, 'I want to live, I want to live, I want to live! I'm having fun, I'm having fun, I'm having fun!' So I told her I was only the boyfriend, but I'd make sure everyone knew she was pretty certain she wanted to live."

Arden had the surgery and went into remission for many months. When the cancer reared its ugly head again, we checked in with Arden once more. She was game for more treatments, but made sure we understood there would be a point when she would tell us no more, and she wanted us to honor her choice when the time came.

EddieMac was only eight when the beginning of the beginning came. He was my goofy, loving, party dog. Always ready to play, he would chase a ball or a stuffed duck for hours, wagging his tail nonstop and wearing a huge silly dog grin. As if overnight, a lemon-sized lump appeared beneath the skin of his chest. The growth was so big and had appeared so quickly that we wasted no time waiting for an appointment. We took him to CSU's after-hours clinic, hoping they could give us another miracle, hoping they could give us many more months with our precious little boy, hoping for a cure.

This time there was no team of doctors, just the on-call oncology resident. She ran what tests she could that night and worked him into the next day's schedule. I took him back to CSU the next morning and left him there for the additional tests, going in to work physically but not mentally, my thoughts never far from the call I was expecting. The call came just a few hours later, from the same resident we had met the night before. I was devastated. There would be no life-extending surgery, no remission, no chance to catch our breath and grow gradually accustomed to his transition. EddieMac also had mast cell cancer, but it was in his spleen and had spread to his lymph system. With radiation and chemotherapy he would have a month or two. Without treatment he would have a few days or, at most, a few weeks.

We brought him home that night and spent time with him, holding him, scratching his ears, playing an endless game of fetch, and asking him if it was time to end the bigger game. The clarity of his answer, the planning of this life of his surprised us.

"I'm on vacation," he told us.

He sent both Jordan and me mental pictures of whirlwind traveling, rushing to catch the ship to the next destination and the one after that. It was a kind of "see the universe in a hundred years" tour.

"I've stayed here longer than I intended, and it's time for me to go. I didn't want to give you time to think about it, time to worry about what to do. I just wanted it to be quick. But I can see how sad you are, and I want to give you more time. I'll take the treatments, I'll stay a little longer, but I don't want to be uncomfortable on my vacation. That's the deal I'll make with you. I'll stay longer for you, and you'll let me go quickly when I say it's time."

EddieMac gave us almost two more months, and in that time we were privileged to see another aspect of his beautiful soul. During those weeks, his tail never stopped wagging and he never lost his wonderful silly grin, but he became more serious, as if he wanted to leave something of himself with everyone he met in the time he had left. Jordan had taught him how to shake hands, and that became his signature greeting. He offered his paw to everyone he came in contact with, sometimes seeking people out in the CSU waiting room. He not only offered them his paw, he also made and held eye contact with them. I watched in amazement as each person who took his paw and met his eyes visibly relaxed, visibly stepped into a moment of peace with him. They invariably returned his silly grin. It was as if he offered his unconditional love and a space of peace along with an old-fashioned doggie hand shake.

Jordan and I are thankful that we were financially able to provide treatment for both Arden and EddieMac, but it has not always been so. Sometimes our animal companions become ill when we simply do not have the resources to seek extensive treatments for them. Many veterinarian hospitals offer low cost care and payment plans to qualifying clients. Some offer aid programs, such as CSU's Companion Care Fund. Whether you can provide treatment for your animal companion or not,

I invite you to consider that your animal companion may have chosen the exact circumstances of his or her transition, including your finances. If you have exhausted all avenues to pay for lifesaving or life-extending care and you cannot afford it, this may be exactly how your animal companion planned it. Even when we listen to our animal's wishes, sometimes we simply cannot let them go, and they know this. Our animal companions take care of us as much as we take care of them during their transitions.

Sometimes when our animal companions become ill, even seriously ill, it may not be the beginning of their transitions. Not long ago, our beautiful boy Cruz became gravely ill. His abdomen was distended and his breathing labored. His legs seemed too weak to adequately support his body. He developed an abscess in his ear and constant nosebleeds. Logically, I thought that he must be ready to transition and that his transition would be very soon. But when I talked with him, he clearly told me he was not ready to transition and even asked me not to let him go.

My own intuition told me that I was losing him, but maybe did not have to. An initial visit to the CSU emergency service gave us only pieces of the puzzle. His blood pressure was very high and the first brief ultrasound showed what could be a mass in his abdomen. We left the hospital with medication for his blood pressure and an appointment for in-depth testing on the following Monday.

Everything I was hearing only led my logical mind to believe I needed to prepare for his transition. And yet his communication did not change.

"I'm really tired Mom," he told me, "but I want to stay with you. Please help me stay."

I was perplexed and beginning to doubt I was receiving his communications clearly. My intuition was still telling me that he could be treated for whatever was making him ill, but the limited facts I had seemed to say he was most likely terminally ill.

I spent the next few days hugging Cruz often and letting him know how very special he is. I talked with him about my confusion. I told him that I wanted to honor his desire to stay, but I was worried that he might not be able to.

On Monday, I drove Cruz to CSU with an odd emotional mix of fear and relief. I waited while the doctors ran blood tests and performed an extensive ultrasound of his abdomen. After a few long hours, the admitting doctor gave me the news. What had looked like a mass on the first ultrasound was actually an enlarged liver and adrenal glands. Further blood work confirmed that Cruz had Cushing's disease, which is serious but not fatal. His adrenal glands were producing far more cortisol than his body needed and this imbalance was making him critically ill. The veterinarian further explained that though Cushing's could not be cured, it could be managed. Cruz could live out a normal and comfortable life.

All the confusion of the last few days cleared as she explained his illness to me. Cruz was right! He wasn't ready to leave. And as sick as he was, there were medications that would allow him to stay and feel better.

Carefully listen to both your animal companion and your intuition. If your animal is ill, even gravely ill, don't be afraid to keep searching until you have the information you need if your instincts tell you this is not "it" and your animal confirms your intuition. It may be that your companion is giving you more time to come to grips with his or her transition. But it may as easily be that your animal is asking for your help to become well again.

If you are listening with your intuition and your heart, as well as with your logical brain, you will not miss the beginning of the beginning. You *will* know when your animal companion is telling you that his or her transition has begun.

Every animal is a unique being who may plan to experience a longer transition time for the lessons the experience will provide, or may simply be done with this life and is ready to move forward quickly. However our animal companions choose to transition, asking them how they want to transition and honoring their wishes with a generous heart will create a space of beauty, love, remembering, and learning for everyone involved.

When you allow yourself to be fully aware of the beginning of your animal companion's transition, you allow time for you and your friend to be together and take care of each other. You allow the time we humans need and our animal companions give us to take stock of the moment before, the moment after, and all the moments in between.

Chapter Four Workbook Exercises

1. Think back to the various endings and beginnings you've experienced in your life. How would they be different if you viewed them not as endings, but purely as beginnings? How would they be different if you viewed them not as endings or even beginnings, but simply as transitions?

2. Think back on your animal companions who have already transitioned. Can you remember the "beginning of the beginning" moment they shared with you? How did they let you know their transition had begun? What difference did that make in your relationship with them?

3. If you have not yet talked with your animal companion about the transition, take time to do that now. What is she or he telling you? How can you best fulfill his or her wishes? How can you best be present during the transition?

CHAPTER FIVE

Celebrating Your Life with Your Animal Companion

Arden and EddieMac

It's mid-morning on a cool spring Saturday. The sky is a brilliant cloudless blue and the air is just crisp enough to make running around an agility field enjoyable for the eight eager pairs of dog and human agility students. I'm holding on to two of our dogs, Cruz and Arden, while Jordan and EddieMac take their turn navigating the dog walk. They both have identical silly grins on their faces, and I can feel my own face moving into that same grin when EddieMac pounces off the bottom of the dog walk and jumps up to snag his reward of string cheese from Jordan.

This is the first class of the beginning agility course we've enrolled EddieMac and Cruz in. All of us are having a wonderful time, even Arden, who is only here to watch and play.

Most of the other dogs are younger than EddieMac, but few of them can match his enthusiasm, his rampant joy to be outside on a beautiful day jumping over jumps, running through tunnels, and getting significant amounts of string cheese. Jordan and I take turns running EddieMac and Cruz over the training courses, and then I hold the two boys while Jordan helps thirteen-year-old Arden go over small jumps and through short tunnels. She has lost some of the spring in her step, but none of her drive to show off. And she loves agility.

Both Jordan and I are taking pictures with our phones. We take pictures of just the dogs, pictures of each other with the dogs, pictures of EddieMac on the dog walk, Arden sitting by a tunnel. We take pictures of all the moments we will want to revisit in the days to come.

The other human students graciously accommodate our desire to digitally capture the day, offering to hold a dog or to take a group picture of the five of us. They all know that EddieMac will likely not finish the six-week course and that Arden's cancer has returned.

I am grateful for these people, all animal lovers, who know that no matter how long we have with our four-legged family members, it is never long enough. I am grateful that they not only hug us and tell us they are sorry, but also laugh with us and play with EddieMac, Arden, and Cruz.

They know that while we are already grieving for what is to come, we are celebrating too. We are celebrating the moment with our beautiful animal companions; we are celebrating our lives together.

Celebrate

To honor, recognize and show appreciation for an event or another being.

What do you think of when you hear the word "celebrate"? Do you see a party in your mind's eye? Or a formal ceremony? A quiet moment under the stars or a family dinner? The word "celebrate" represents a much more versatile concept than any definition you might read in a dictionary. Not every celebration takes place as a party or a ceremony or even at a specific time. You can celebrate the beauty of nature by filling your home with plants. You can celebrate music by learning how to play an instrument.

To celebrate something or someone is also to honor that thing or being, to show respect and appreciation.

If you want to learn how to truly celebrate, you only have to watch your animal companions. They celebrate their human and animal family members with love and play. Working animals for whom the work is natural and calls to them celebrate the work with keen attention and joy. Just watch a herding dog circling sheep and you will see what I mean. Almost all animals celebrate dinnertime with great enthusiasm. Our animals live in the moment and lack the human fear of looking silly. They are excellent teachers of celebration and honoring.

We humans often have a far harder time living in the moment than our animal companions. We have work to think of, meals to plan, car pools to arrange, and any number of items that call for our attention in our day-to-day lives. We may remember to celebrate life and honor our loved ones for a time and then let the idea be pushed to the back of our minds by more demanding responsibilities and commitments.

The beginning of your animal companion's transition can serve as a reminder to stop and live in the moment, to celebrate and honor all the moments you have with your dear friend.

When you know that your animal companion's transition has begun, no matter how much time you and your friend have left, take time to sit and talk with them and find out how they want to celebrate your remaining time together. The answers will be as varied as the animals you are talking with.

Some will want to play more if they are able, or even to continue the work they love as long as they can. Some may want to spend quiet time with you or go for walks or rides with you. Some may want special food treats, and most will love the idea of more food in general as long as they can still eat. If you are pursuing treatment for your animal companion's illness, check with your veterinarian before increasing exercise or food. But in most cases, you will know how much of anything is enough for you and your companion.

When Arden's transition began, I sat with her and asked her what we could do to make our time together special. In her pert and no-nonsense style she told me that she wanted lots more food, and fun food at that, not just regular everyday food. Her very clear goal was to go out fat and sassy. She also said she missed the long walks we used to take together and asked if we could go for walks again.

I had not taken Arden for walks in a few years because she could not keep up with the other two dogs and she was always spent at the end of a walk. I felt awful when she requested walks again and wished I had found a way to give her something she enjoyed so much before the thought of her transition pushed me to it. I apologized to Arden, telling her how sorry I was to have left her out of walks. She immediately let me know that she didn't want me to waste time feeling bad about what I had done or not done in the past. She much preferred I put my energy into taking her on walks now.

Jordan and I found a used baby stroller at a garage sale the next day. After refitting the stroller to accommodate a canine passenger and dubbing it the Ardiemobile,

Arden was back out on long walks. Repeatedly, she let us know how much she enjoyed her special stroller and those walks. She often growled at our two boy dogs if they tried to get in her Ardiemobile. We took picture after picture of Arden in her stroller on walks, and those pictures are some of our most treasured possessions.

The lesson Arden taught me about taking her for walks is an important one. We humans live in a world too easily filled with regrets over past choices. Those regrets can be especially crippling when they are centered on animals and people who are transitioning.

Our animals live in the world of now, a world where regrets are useless and only get in the way of what can be. Our animal companions ask us not to waste time worrying about what we did or did not do for them. They would rather we put our energy into what we can do with and for them now. They ask us to put aside anything that gets in the way of celebrating our lives together in the magical moment of now.

Another request our animal companions make of us is to let go of our preconceived notions of how we should celebrate together. We may feel that we should be emotionally strong around our animal companions and others, even though we literally ache from the grief our animal's transition is causing us. We may feel that we should put on a light-hearted face for everyone else. Or we may feel the need to be especially solemn and reverent as our animal companion transitions. We may feel that a desire to laugh or be silly is inappropriate during such a serious time. Both being sad when someone we love is transitioning *and* feeling the need to take a break from that sadness with laughter and play are natural expressions of the human experience. Neither is right or wrong. Our animals challenge us to let go of our "shoulds" and simply be with how we feel. We celebrate and honor them equally with our tears and our laughter. They ask us for authenticity. They want to be with who and how we truly are in the moment.

Sometimes the universe gives us unexpected opportunities to celebrate with our companions. That ordinary trip to the store, walk in the pasture, or appointment with the veterinarian can suddenly provide an opening for an extraordinary experience.

In the December before Arden left her body, Jordan and I, along with Arden, Cruz, and Capo, went on a road trip to visit my family in Alabama. Our plan was to stop at Dauphin Island in Alabama to see the Gulf of Mexico and let the dogs sniff in the aromas of the ocean. A wrong turn took us away from our intended destination and brought us instead to a quiet and secluded cove of Mobile Bay. We were the only ones there on that overcast Christmas Eve, and we took the opportunity to let all three dogs play on the beach. Arden was ecstatic. Over and over she told us, "I can smell the world!"

We spent over an hour there, watching and video-taping while our fourteen-year-old girl, in the last stages of her cancer, chased gentle waves on unsteady but determined legs, stopping only to sniff the newest thing the waves uncovered.

Allow yourself to stop and take in those unexpected opportunities to celebrate with your animal companion. Allow yourself to observe and commemorate even the smallest moments that bring you and your animal joy.

Most of us love to take pictures of our animal companions. We pose them in costumes or with other family members, we sneak up on them while they're sleeping, or we set the stage carefully and snap dozens of shots hoping to capture them doing that one thing that is the cutest or most beautiful thing we've ever seen. Some of us continue the photographic journey even when our animal companions are terminally ill, while others cannot bear the thought of capturing a lasting image of our cherished companions when they are not vibrant and healthy.

As always, you must celebrate your animal companion in the manner that feels right for the two of you. And I invite you to consider that your animal's soul may shine most brightly as they near the time of their transition and take on something of both this life and the one to come. This time of transition is as vital a part of your life with your animal companion as the day you brought him or her home. It is a part of your journey together, a part of your learning and growing together.

The pictures you take of this part of your journey can serve as a record of your souls creating together a space of beauty and love in which one gives room for the other to transition from life to life with peace and joy.

Listen to the lessons your animal gives you in the quiet moments and in the silly and perhaps even ridiculous moments. There is beauty in every moment of your life with your special animal companion. Honor and *celebrate* them all!

Chapter Five Workbook Exercises

1. Reflect on the word "celebrate." What images does it bring to mind for you? Think of a time that you have celebrated something or someone without a ceremony or a festivity. What was that like for you?

2. If you have not already done so, ask your animal companion how they would like to celebrate your life together. What answers did they give you?

3. Keep a journal of how you and your animal companion are celebrating. Include both your planned activities and the spontaneous special moments.

4. Put together a photo book or collage of you and your animal companion. Keep taking pictures now if you are comfortable with the idea. Talk with your animal companion about what is special to you in each photo.

CHAPTER SIX

Giving Your Animal Companion Permission to Transition

EddieMac

The late afternoon light drifts through the windows of the CSU family room in lazy fits as passing clouds alternately block and reveal the sun. I stare at the haphazard patterns the light makes on the armrest of the chair I'm sitting in as if they will tell me how I came to be here today, sitting in this chair in the family room of a veterinarian hospital, waiting for the doctors to stabilize my little boy and bring him to me so that I can let him go. As if there is a message in the play of light and shadow that will make sense of it all. He was doing better; he ate a little this morning! And even if he hated taking all those pills I forced down his throat for the last week and the fluids we injected beneath his skin for the last three nights, it was all right, because it would make him well. And I so desperately want my beloved EddieMac to be well again. But his body will not be well again. This blending of soul and personality and beautiful cocker spaniel body that I know as EddieMac will not last another day, with or without euthanasia.

I stand, leaving the muted light and its secretive patterns behind to pace the room. I wish again that I was not alone here, but I know that my friends are all too far away to come and be with me at this last minute, this last minute that arrived with no notice or warning. When I left with EddieMac for the two-hour drive to Fort Collins, I thought I would be bringing him home with me. I thought the doctors would give us yet another treatment adjustment that would ease his labored breathing and give us yet another day. I did not know when I left that the tumor in his throat had grown large enough to block his trachea, hinder his breathing, and deprive his body of oxygen. I did not know. Now I do and this knowledge dazes me, leaves me unable to think past the moment when the doctor told me my little boy would not live through the night.

Then I remember this morning when EddieMac obediently swallowed the pills I had given him to keep his body going just a little longer. I had petted his head and told him what a good boy he was. I'd been pleased he had taken the pills without his usual resistance. Just as I turned from him, going off to do something I can no longer remember, I heard the unmistakable sound of vomiting. I turned back and saw my sweet little boy, his face

*alight with his silly dog grin, his tail wagging, a
pile of honey-coated pills lying in front of him. His
tail still wagging, he sat down and offered me his
paw. I heard him clearly in my head.*

*"I told you I wasn't taking any more pills, Mom.
Can I go now?"*

*This memory floods my mind and draws me back
to the chair and the drifting light which is no
longer drifting but now seems to stream in with
steady purpose. I fall into the chair. I know the
secret, the secret I have hidden from myself. I
didn't keep my promise to EddieMac. I have kept
him with me longer than he wants, longer than
he is comfortable. He has been in pain and I have
kept giving him pills as if we were two thieves
stealing time, as if I could cover my eyes and play
a game of pretend in which he is well and happy.
He has been asking me to let him go, and I have
refused to hear him.*

*I have only a moment to let this unwelcome truth
sink in before they bring EddieMac to me. His
oncologist is carrying him and a nurse comes in
with her, rolling a portable oxygen machine into
the room. EddieMac is breathing easier now and
for a moment I forget my newfound secret. Maybe
I can take him home. Maybe we do have yet another*

day. The doctor reads my frantic thoughts in my eager expression and shakes her head as she gently places EddieMac in my lap.

"I know he looks better," she says, "but it's only because we've been giving him oxygen. It won't last. You know this; he knows this."

I hold my little boy close as she gives me instructions on how to use the portable oxygen and tells me to take as long as I need with him. Then she leaves the room.

The sound of the door closing behind her steadies me, allows me to mentally step into a space of calm and become present to the beautiful dog I hold in my arms. I look at EddieMac and I see him, really see him, as I have not allowed myself to do over the last two weeks. He has grown so thin that his ribs and the tumor beneath the muscles of his neck stand out with clear definition. His soul still shines through his eyes, but those eyes are dull with pain and effort. His fur is dull as well, and his muzzle is streaked with gray that wasn't there just a few weeks ago. Arden has taught me about regrets and I will not waste time with them now. They will wait for later. Now I must give my little boy relief and peace.

EddieMac and I spend long minutes in that sunlit chair, communing together. He snuggles with me, offering me his paw in a handshake and his love in a gentle doggie kiss. I tell him he is my special boy and I thank him for being my dog, my friend. We reminisce on our life together, the dog shows we've gone to, the games we've played, and how he was named for a Denver Broncos' football player because he always bounced right back up from a puppy tackle.

I tell him I am grateful to have known him. I tell him how much I love him. I tell him it is okay for him to go now, to leave his body. I tell him that I will hold him and wish him bon voyage as he leaves to catch the next ship.

Permission

To give consent to another, to allow them to do or not do a given action.

Complete

To be whole, to leave nothing lacking.

The word "permission" can have a rigid feel to it. It may paint a mental picture of a student asking for a hall pass or a child asking permission to go on a field trip. In this mental picture, it is easy to believe that the student will not go into the hall and the child will not go on the field trip without permission. In that context it seems almost absurd to think of our animal companions asking for our permission to transition and waiting on us to give it to them. If it were that simple, no beloved animal companion would ever transition.

But just as the student may very well end up in the hall without permission and the child may forge a signature and go on the field trip with none the wiser, so too our animals do not wait on formal permission to leave their bodies.

In most cases, asking for permission is really asking for agreement and acceptance. Unless we are physically held captive, we rarely need literal permission to do something, but it is always easier to take actions when we have the agreement and acceptance of those close to us, those we love and respect.

Our animal companions are no different. They want our acceptance and agreement, our permission, especially when they are transitioning. Transitioning from life to life is a much easier choice for our animals, but even with their clearer connection to all that has been and will be, transitioning is still a difficult process. They seek our support, spiritually as well as physically. When they ask us for permission to transition, they are asking for this support. When we give them our permission, we are saying that we accept their choice, we accept their transition. We are saying we will support them.

The animals who have chosen to be with us love us unconditionally, without reservation or judgment. Our well-being is also important to them during this process and if they can, they will give us time to come to terms with their transition. EddieMac was ready, even eager, to transition when he was first diagnosed with mast cell cancer. He graciously gave us the time we needed to accept his transition. And even when I held on to him longer than he wanted, he still waited for me to find a space of acceptance and peace. Our animal companions take care of us as much as we take care of them, and they want to know that we are ready for their transitions, that we accept this new phase of their souls' lives.

There are many ways you can give your animal companion permission to transition. It can be as simple as saying, "It's okay to go," if it is a sudden transition. Or you and your animal may want to have a ceremony together. That ceremony can be as formal or as informal as you want. It may be as simple as sitting outside in a favorite spot. If there is time, ask your animal how they would like to receive your permission and listen to their answer with your heart. Your companion may only need permission from you, or they may want permission from other family members as well.

Another aspect of giving your animal companion permission to transition is becoming complete with the life you have shared together. What does it mean for something or someone to be complete? It means lacking nothing, being whole and entire. To complete something is to make it whole and entire. How do we do this with a life? We say whatever there is in our hearts to say to the other soul. We may tell them we love them, we may thank them or acknowledge them in some special way, and we may ask for or give forgiveness. If you are angry (and being angry over the transition of a loved one is normal) you may want to talk about your anger and find a space of forgiveness together.

As you and your animal companion complete your life together, you may also find that one or both of you want to discuss what is next. Who will you be for each other after the transition? How and when will you reconnect after the transition? Allow room for these conversations. Play with the notion that you and your companion may have a relationship after the transition, that your two souls may reconnect after he or she has transitioned, even though you are still in physical form. My beautiful Roxy told me that there is no finality, only the next thing to be learned. We humans have a harder time comprehending the eternal now that all souls live in. There is no finality, no ending in this eternal now—only endless possibilities.

When you complete your life together with your animal companion you are bringing your relationship with your companion into a state of being whole and entire. You are creating a space in which you and your dear friend can move forward to the next phase of your souls' eternal now together.

Giving them permission to transition is not just for your animal. You are also giving yourself permission to let them go. We live in a world of rapid medical advancements, not just for humans, but for animals as well. Injuries and illnesses that were hopeless just ten years ago can now be treated and the animal can sometimes be restored to a healthy state. It is easy to become swept up in the desire and need to pursue the latest treatment, the newest pill that will give you more time or even stop whatever is threatening to end your companion's life. It is easy to want to hold it at bay long enough for you to find the next stopgap measure that could give you time enough to find a cure for your beloved companion. It is a natural part of being human to hold on to life, sometimes at all costs. We can drive ourselves mad with guilt, desperation, and exhaustion as we seek that next new pill or treatment. In the process, we sometimes lose sight of our companion's desires. We also may lose the beauty of the time we have left with them.

EddieMac's tumors initially responded well to chemotherapy and radiation, shrinking dramatically. And then the radiation began to irritate his esophagus and his irritated esophagus affected his stomach. Soon he could not keep food down. We had to stop his cancer treatments and his tumors began to grow again. I became panicked, believing that I wasn't doing enough to save his life, and I became fixated on relieving the radiation side effects so EddieMac's cancer treatments could continue.

By that last day when he told me, "No more," I was giving him pills to help his system keep down pills that would prepare his system to work with the pills that might ease his esophagus enough to allow him to eat and then continue with radiation and chemotherapy. I was acting out of fear and guilt that I was not fulfilling my responsibilities and promises as his human companion to keep him safe, to keep him well. In acting on this gut level need to keep him alive, I lost sight of EddieMac. I filled our last days with pills and injections. I forgot to just be with him and love him, to let him go while he was comfortable as he had asked me to do.

When I gave EddieMac permission to go, I gave myself permission to let him go. I gave myself permission to let go of my frantic quest to keep him alive at all costs, and I gained the opportunity to connect with my beautiful boy soul to soul. Instead of focusing on the next physical issue to be solved, I gained the opportunity to see EddieMac again.

There is a time to pursue the next treatment and there is a time to let go. Talk with your animal's doctor and listen carefully, then talk with your animal and listen with your heart. Only you and your animal companion can choose when is the time to let go, but don't lose sight of your animal's wishes. When you give yourself permission to let your animal transition, you are also giving yourself permission to let go of any guilt you may be holding about your companion's condition.

You are allowing yourself to let go of everything that keeps you from being present with and for your animal companion.

I will never forget sitting in that waiting room chair with EddieMac. I can still recall the feeling of my fear and panicky need to hang on to him draining away and being replaced with strength and peace as I gave him permission to leave and we completed our life together. Minutes later, I called on that peace and strength as I sat in the circle of his transition, holding his head in my lap while his doctor administered the reddish fluid that would free his soul from his body. I continued to tell him it was okay to go as his heart beat slowed and then stopped. And when his soul shook free of his body, I could feel his joy flow through me as he soared on to his next adventure. When I gave him permission to go, when I gave myself permission to let him go, I made room to be present with him during his transition. I allowed myself space to feel his joy and to know that *he* had not come to an end.

As you give your animal companion permission to transition and give yourself permission to let them go, you are also creating and holding a space to feel their joy through your grief, to know that they continue. You are allowing room to feel the magic of a conscious transition.

Chapter Six Workbook Exercises

1. Describe what giving another soul permission to transition means to you. Ask your animal companion what it means to him or her. How are your meanings the same? How are they different?

2. Is your animal companion asking for permission to transition now? Describe how this makes you feel. How can you give yourself permission to let your companion transition? How would your animal companion like to receive permission? How would you like to give yourself permission?

3. How would you like to complete your life with your animal companion? Is there anything you would like to tell your animal to make your life together complete? Are there other family members who would like to participate in this process?

CHAPTER SEVEN

When Your Animal Companion Transitions from Life to Life

Sony

The late summer sun heats the earth around me and the earth returns the heat to the sun in shimmering waves. A fine sheen of sweat coats my face, and cicadas buzz their song of life from the distant bushes. My reluctant footsteps disturb grasshoppers resting in the sparse, thirsty lawn I'm crossing and they leap in front of me like messengers hurrying to the bordering trees carrying news of my impending arrival.

Some remote part of my brain makes note of all these small details of the summer afternoon I'm walking through with detached clarity. But the largest part of my consciousness is filled with the feel of the frail and furry body of the dog I'm carrying to the trees, clutched to my shoulder with begrudging arms that do not want to let her go. It is as if I am two people: One can feel, hear, and see the normal, everyday activity around me; the other cannot. The one, oblivious to everyday activity, can feel only the warmth of the dog I'm holding, see only her face so close to mine, hear only the sound of her tired heartbeat.

Sony has just turned twelve years old and she is not terminally ill. No injury, no tumor threatens her life. Instead, her joy and spirit are being drained away with aching slowness as her soul struggles to find ease and purchase in a body that can no longer support it, a body that once moved with swift grace at her soul's command but has now become little more than a trap.

I know this because she has shown me this, has let me feel what life in this body is for her now. Now that she is losing her sense of smell and she can no longer hear. Now that her one remaining eye is filling with the unbearable pressure of glaucoma and her head pounds in rhythm with her slowing heartbeat. Now that her diabetes can no longer be controlled and her deteriorating hips can no longer be counted on to support her shrinking weight.

Sony is twelve, not so old, not so young. There is no one thing wrong with her and she has asked me to help her leave her body. Until last night, I could not tell her yes. For days I have been as trapped by my indecision as she is by her body, unable to see past either my need to keep her with me or her gentle but persistent request to be set free. I have only just remembered how to communicate with animals, with Sony, and my mind does not trust the communication my soul knows I have received. Yesterday, I called my mentor, a professional animal communicator, and she received the same message from Sony. Still uncertain, I made the appointment for Sony's veterinarian to come to our house, telling myself I could always cancel, always change my mind, always keep Sony with me until the choice is no choice at all, but merely a fact.

Until last night, when I sat with Sony in the cool of the night under glimmering stars in a moonless sky and opened my soul to hers, asking her to let me feel what she felt. And she did, letting me feel the pain in her hips and head, the hunger and nausea that never abated no matter how much or little she ate, the countless aches and pains that nagged at her, sapping her strength one slow, irretrievable drop at a time, and the constant longing of her soul to stretch free and dance again. I knew then I would do as she asked.

Now, as I carry Sony across the lawn and into the shade of the old apple trees where the veterinarian waits for us, I can feel my resolve faltering. I hold on to the memory of what Sony has shown me like a talisman and somehow find the strength to sit down on the blanket beside the veterinarian. I shift Sony to my lap and she leans into me, reassuring me, sending silent messages of confirmation as I listen to the doctor explain what will happen next.

I am calm as I watch the doctor swab Sony's front leg with alcohol. I am still calm when the doctor gives Sony the sedative that will drop her into physical unconsciousness, and I smile when Sony meets my gaze with her own and places her paw on my arm. This is what she wants. In this moment I am steadfast in my choice, sure that I am giving her the gift of freedom, and this feeling sings through my soul, bolstering me. But when Sony folds to the ground as the sedative takes hold, I begin to shake. That wondrous feeling of certainty flees in the face of my fear. I clutch Sony's unconscious body and sob. I say nothing as the doctor gives Sony the final injection, the one that will still her physical heart, but in my mind, I am screaming. Oh God and angels above, what have I done? I cannot take this back; I cannot undo this and make another choice! I have taken Sony's life as surely as if I had given her the injection myself and I am wracked with disbelief and guilt.

Then, just as Sony's breathing ceases and mine becomes ragged with grief, I see her. I see her only from the corners of my physical eyes, but I see her clearly with the eyes of my soul. I see her soul lifting from her body like a glorious golden bird rising from a long sleep, unfurling her wings, testing them, and finding them strong once more. I see her hover near me for a moment, enfolding me in her wings, and I am flooded with warm love and comfort. Then I see her soar into the sky, spiraling upwards on the outstretched wings of her soul, turning and diving only to turn and wheel upwards again. I see her dancing.

Life
A time frame designated with a physical beginning and ending that a soul experiences on Earth or any other plane of existence.

The spark that animates our physical beings into motion.

Conscious Transition Term: Circle of Transition
The people or animals who are present, physically or mentally, during an animal's ultimate moment of transition.

There are many definitions for the word "life" and several more idiomatic phrases containing this powerful word. The word "life" represents a concept so enormous in our world that even with numerous definitions for it, we still only catch a glimpse of what life is. It is a word with both universal and individual meaning for each being.

Life is what each of us is busy living right here, right now. We are all souls living a life together. Life is also that spark, that essence that animates our physical bodies, making us who we are. This concept of life holds true for our animal companions too. Their bodies are animated by the life force of their souls and they are all here living their lives alongside us as we live ours.

When our animals transition they are moving that animating spark from their bodies into a state of energy. They are leaving this life and moving into the next, whatever form that life may take. This is what we humans call death. The animals see this process as being more like birth. They are breaking free of the body that holds them, from which their soul has been nurtured, and moving into another state of existence.

This moment when our animal's soul leaves the body we recognize and love can be the most difficult moment of all—even when we see this ultimate moment of our animal companion's transition as a birth and not a death, even when we have gone through all the steps of a conscious transition and we *know* this is what our animal wants, even when we *know* that our cherished companion will not end.

There will be no turning back from this ultimate moment, no second chance, no time to reconsider. You may experience doubt or fear, anger, or intense sorrow.

And you may feel nothing at all, only to be swamped with a rush of emotions minutes, hours, or even days later.

In this ultimate moment of transition, you will need the comfort and reassurance of your beloved animal companion as much as he or she will need yours. Let go of any concern you may have about leaning on your animal for emotional support. Your companion's body may be frail and failing, but your dear friend's soul is as whole and strong as ever. Talk with your animal, let them know how you feel, and ask them to help you.

In a conscious transition, at this ultimate moment of transition, your role will be to create and hold a space of love and peace in which your beloved animal companion may move with ease and joy from this awareness to the next, from being a soul surrounding and immersed in a biological body to a soul free of restraint, truly existing in the eternal now, riding the waves of the universe.

Stepping into this role may sound like a complicated and imposing task but it really is very simple. Love your animal, feel your love for him or her, visualize this love surrounding you and your animal and holding you both. Even if you cannot speak, communicate with your dear friend. Send your love and your acceptance of this transition to your companion. Give yourself permission to feel whatever emotions are there for you. Allow them to be. Waste no time on trying to get this right. Just be present with and for your animal companion.

The ability to create and hold this space of love and acceptance for your animal companion's transition is innately within you. If you question whether or not you are strong enough, go ahead and question! You are strong enough; your very vulnerability gives you strength. You cannot get this wrong. Just allow who you are and your love for your beloved friend to be.

In sudden transitions, such as catastrophic injuries, you may feel that you don't have time to prepare yourself for creating and holding a space of love. Everything may be so rushed, so abrupt, that you can barely think, much less achieve the presence to send love and peace to your animal. Again, draw on your vulnerability and allow your emotions to be whatever they are. You will not get it wrong. Your love for your animal companion will shine through no matter how rushed, scared, or even angry you may feel.

If you cannot be with your animal companion when he or she transitions, you can still create and hold space for the transition. Send your love to your animal, see him or her in your mind, and picture your companion surrounded by your love and acceptance.

When I took EddieMac to CSU for his labored breathing, I thought I would be bringing him home with me. My husband, Jordan, chose to stay home with our other two dogs and wait for the two of us to return. He was devastated when I called him and told him EddieMac would not be coming back with me. We didn't have time for him to drive the two hours from our house to Fort Collins to be with us. EddieMac could not wait that long. I did not know how long I would need to let the reality of what I must do next set in, so I could only tell Jordan that EddieMac would transition within the next hour.

Jordan had only known EddieMac for a short time, but he had come to love him as much as I did and was heartbroken not to be with EddieMac when he transitioned. Jordan asked EddieMac how he could help him, even though he could not be physically present with him. In his physical form, EddieMac was deaf, and even though he had watched Jordan play the guitar many times, he had never heard the music. EddieMac asked Jordan to play his guitar when he transitioned so he could hear the music before he left on his greater journey.

Jordan lit a candle, pulled out his guitar, and played song after song, sending his music and his love to EddieMac as he transitioned. When EddieMac left his body, I felt him transition. I felt his exuberant joy to be free of his physical limitations and I felt his wonder at being able to hear music again. I was perplexed by that thought, sure I was making it up. There was no music playing in the secluded waiting room of the veterinarian hospital. It was not until I had made the long drive home and was at last in the comforting embrace of my family that I knew where the music had come from. And then I knew that Jordan had been there with me in the circle of EddieMac's transition, even though he was physically over one hundred miles away.

Sometimes our animal companions transition when we are not with them, and we do not know they are going to transition. We may be on vacation and our companion is at home or a boarding facility. We may be at work or any number of other places when our companion transitions from life to life without warning. This can leave us shattered with guilt and remorse at our perceived failure to be there for our cherished companion. Know that your animal companion may have chosen to transition in this manner, may have chosen to spare you from making a choice you were not ready to make.

Know that it is still possible for you to aid in your companion's transition. On a universal level, time is little more than a manmade device to aid us in understanding the world we live in. On the universal level, we all live in the eternal now. What has been, what is, and what will be are all already, now, in this moment. Your animal's transition may have been two days ago or two years ago, and yet it is also now. You can step into the eternal now and create and hold a space of love and peace for your animal companion.

You may want to plan a ceremony. You could light candles or surround yourself with your companion's cherished possessions and let your companion know that you are meeting her or him at the moment of transition in the eternal now. Then visualize your dear friend surrounded by your love and visualize your companion's transition aided by your love. Know that your animal companion feels your presence, feels your love, and will transition without fear or loneliness. Know that your animal will know you are there and that he or she is transitioning through your love. Know that the arms of your soul are holding the soul of your friend through the transition.

It is that simple when we allow ourselves to see the world through the eyes of our souls.

Our role in our animal companions' transitions will always remain the same, no matter what the circumstances of their transitions may be. This role we play is the fulfillment of the promise we make to our animals to always take care of them. As daunting as it can seem, we will always be able to play this role, always be able to fulfill this promise.

Our role does not vary, but the circumstances of our animal companions' transitions can take many forms. In sudden transitions, you may be limited in your choices, but when you and your animal companion are facing a terminal illness or the inevitable conclusion of the body's aging process, you will usually have time to plan the circumstances of your companion's transition.

If there is time, and in most cases there will be, talk with your animal companion about his or her transition. Ask your animal how, when, and where they would like to transition. Ask your animal who they would like to include in the circle of their transition. Remember, it does not matter if these people or animals can be physically present. They can still aid in your companion's transition.

Allow yourself to share your worries, fears, and concerns with your dear friend. Your animal companion already knows how hard this will be for you. Listen to the communication in whatever form your animal sends it. You may hear them in your mind or you may see mental pictures of their wishes. If you need further reassurance that the path you are on is what your companion wants, you may experience your animal's physical discomfort or you may feel a sense of peace. Your animal will find a way to let you know how and when they want to transition and will give you a message of comfort and reassurance.

A week after Arden asked me to let her go, but before I had made the appointment for her transition, I often found myself thinking the words, "I'm so sick and tired; I just want to go home." I had no idea why these words were coming to my mind. I wasn't sick, I was seldom tired, and I was often already home when I would have the thought. One day, after I had thought these words many times, I looked up and saw Arden watching me. In her typical direct fashion, she "told" me, "I know you're not tired and sick. I am! I'm ready to leave this body. Are you ready to help me?"

I knew it was time for Arden and me to plan her transition from life to life.

Our emotions can sometimes cloud our ability to hear our animals' messages. If you have doubts about the messages you are receiving or feel you are not receiving anything at all, take time to let your emotions be. Give yourself space to cry. Give yourself space to be scared, angry, or uncertain. Acknowledging your emotions, giving them room to be without judgment, will give you freedom to be present with your animal companion.

If you still have doubts or feel that you cannot connect with your companion, have a professional animal communicator speak with your animal. This second opinion can help calm your fears and doubt about the communications you are receiving.

Your animal companion may have concerns too. Ask your companion if he or she has any questions or worries. If you have chosen euthanasia, talk with them about the procedure. Tell them what to expect, what the veterinarian will do to free them from their body.

Talk with your veterinarian in advance as well. If your veterinarian offers it, you can choose to let your animal transition at home. If you choose to take your animal companion into the veterinarian's office you may want to ask for a secluded room where you can take your time with your animal companion away from the regular patients. Most veterinarians will give animals a sedative before they administer the euthanasia drug.

This is by far the preferred method because a transition without the sedative can be abrupt and disturbing. Ask your veterinarian in advance how they perform a euthanasia procedure. If they do not give a sedative first, ask if they will make an exception.

Some veterinarian hospitals will have counselors on staff who can be with you and your animal when they leave their body. Do not hesitate to call on this service if it is available. These people are trained to aid you and your companion in this difficult time.

One of the most personal and difficult choices you will make is whether to be physically present or not when your animal is euthanized. Being present when your animal companion leaves their body can be both gut-wrenching and comforting. It is not necessary to be physically present to aid your animal with the transition, but it can often allow you to be more complete with your animal's transition. When you and your animal are creating a conscious transition, it is important to discuss this with your companion. You may feel that your emotions will disturb your animal, or you may not want to remember the sight of your animal companion's lifeless body. Be honest with your animal. In a conscious transition you will choose together what is right for the two of you.

From personal experience, I would invite you to consider being present at this time. I have been present for each of my animal companion's transitions except one, and that is the only one I regret. Each time I have watched the moment when my dear animals left their bodies, I have been left feeling more certain than ever that the spirit, the being I love, was not that body, only housed by it. I have felt their souls move from a place of pain and restriction to a place of freedom and ease, and I have been comforted and sustained by the experience each time.

You and your animal companion may also choose a natural transition without euthanasia. This is a deeply personal choice between you and your companion. In a natural transition, you may be called on to offer a higher level of medical care for your companion in order to keep them comfortable until they transition. If you and your animal have chosen a natural transition, talk extensively with your veterinarian about the kind of care your friend will need. Some veterinarian hospitals offer pet hospice services. With these services, you will have support from trained veterinarian caregivers as you and your animal prepare for the transition. You may also find a pet hospice service valuable when you and your animal have chosen euthanasia. A good pet hospice service will help you keep your companion comfortable at home during their last days in their body.

There are many different ways for your animal companion to transition from life to life. There is no right or wrong way to proceed. Trust that you and your companion will choose what is best for the two of you. Communicate with your dear friend and trust in the communication you receive. Your animal companion will tell you what they wish, you have only to listen with your heart and soul.

The ultimate moment of transition is both the most difficult and the most beautiful moment of your animal companion's transition. Your friend will break free of pain and suffering, and you will touch the eternal fabric of the universe. You will give your companion the most selfless gift any being can give another as you put aside your own grief and pain to allow space for your cherished friend to find ease and peace.

Chapter Seven Workbook Exercises

1. Consider the definition and concept of life. Write out your own definition of life.

2. Ask your animal companion what life means to him or her. Write out your companion's definition of life.

3. Consider the role you will play in creating and holding the space for your animal companion's transition. Talk with your companion about this role. How best can you fulfill this role for your companion?

4. Do you have animal companions who have transitioned suddenly when you could not be with them? If so, consider how you can meet them in the eternal now and aid in their transition.

CHAPTER EIGHT

Conscious Transitions in Sudden Losses

Kobe

I drive the car through the soft glow of a waking day without conscious thought, stopping on red, going on green and making the correct turns without actually seeing them. I am driving to the emergency veterinarian clinic and my thoughts are filled with Kobe, my beautiful six-month-old cocker spaniel puppy. Just yesterday he was playing with his littermate, running with wild exuberance, tackling his sister, Trinket, and dodging her counter pounce. Just yesterday he was a silly puppy, bursting with energy, his agile and strong body responding to all the requests of his soul to run, play, leap, pounce, and give his love to all around him with the enthusiasm of a young puppy, new to this life. Today is different. Today he is only breathing with the help of a ventilator. Today his body is shutting down, one organ at a time. Today his red blood cells are rupturing and he is in shock. He may last another hour or he may only last a few more minutes.

My thoughts have an indistinct quality, as if they are not mine, as if I am watching a movie and am a character in that movie at the same time. I do not really know what happened between yesterday and today. I would like to rewind this movie and watch again, with great care, because I have missed something crucial.

My memory serves up the basic facts. Yesterday both Trinket and Kobe were fine until late afternoon, when they both began to vomit. I took them to the emergency veterinarian clinic, even laughing that these sudden illnesses always happened on weekends. I wasn't worried, not then. I waited while the doctor ran the same tests on both of them. No poison; no disease. But there was an abnormal amount of bacteria in their digestive systems. What had they eaten? Had I given them something new? Had they gotten into anything? I could not think of anything. I am so careful with my babies! They both received the same veterinarian care and now Trinket is back to normal and Kobe is leaving his body. I cannot connect these dots. I cannot understand how Trinket slept peacefully beside me last night while Kobe was losing the battle for his life.

I watched Trinket sleep and called the veterinarian clinic through the night, expecting to hear that

Kobe was better with each call, hearing instead that he continued to become weaker. Over and over, I sifted through the day's events, like a miner desperately sifting through a bare and used pan of dirt just one more time. But I could not unearth why a six-month-old puppy was dying. I had helped animals transition before; I knew the peace they experienced from leaving a failing body. But how in the name of all that is sacred and holy can that be true for a puppy? Old and terminally ill animals, yes, that I could understand, but not my sweet puppy! How could he be healthy one day and leaving the next? Where was the plan in this? I could find no plan, no reason. I finally fell into a restless sleep, wrapped in the guilt of my failure to keep this precious little one safe, hoping I would wake to find it all a dream.

But the morning came and the call that awakened me scattered all my hopes.

"Hello, is this Andrea? I'm so sorry. Kobe is dying. He doesn't have much longer. Do you want to see him, or do you want us to euthanize him for you?" I knew, in my rational mind, that the veterinary receptionist was being kind, but I wanted to scream at her, "No! He's my baby! I want to see him! Please let him live until I can get there!"

95

I didn't scream; I didn't cry. I just quietly thanked her and told her I would be there as soon as I could.

My eyes are still dry now, as I park the car in front of the emergency clinic. My feet are steady as I walk to the entrance but my hand shakes as I open the glass door that is somehow heavier than it was last night. I am grateful for the receptionist now. She does not question why I am here, does not ask me to wait while she helps other clients. She only leads me in silence to my baby.

And then I see Kobe. He is so small on the metal table. Too small. His glossy black chest is rising and falling in time with the raspy cadence of the ventilator. His beautiful brown eyes are open and glazed. He cannot see me. There is a steady stream of blood from his nose and mouth and his gums are white beneath the smear of red. I hear the sound of sobbing and know that it is me when I feel the receptionist put her arm around me, offering me comfort. I shrug off her comfort. I do not deserve it. Somehow, I have caused this. I have done something to kill my baby puppy and I must face this bitter reality alone. I take a step towards Kobe and place a hesitant hand on his rear leg. His fur is soft to my touch, his leg oddly warm, but there is a fragile feel to him, as if his soul is connected to his body by the thinnest of threads and waits only for a thought to break free.

At first I cannot sense Kobe's soul, but then I do and I know that he is almost free. I do not want to face him; I am not ready for the condemnation he will surely have for me. But I cannot resist the steady pull of his soul as he reaches out to me.

"Mom, I can't stay in this body. It's broken and I'm sorry. Can I go? Will you be okay?"

I hear his sorrow, his concern, and I am astounded. I have so many questions, but I know that in this moment I must be present for my baby. I can only do as he asks of me.

"Yes," I tell him, "you can go. I will hold you and love you. I'm sorry too. You are so special to me, and I will always remember my darling little Kobe puppy."

I ignore the tubes and the IV lines and the blood. I pick up my little puppy boy and I hold him close. I cuddle him to me and I bathe him in my tears. While the doctor pushes that reddish fluid through his IV line, I tell him again how special he is, how loved he is.

His soul rips free of the last tether that holds him to his ruined body. I lose my resolve when Kobe leaves his body and give in to my grief and guilt. I can no longer feel his soul near me and I accept this. It is my punishment for failing him.

I stumble through the fog of my emotions to my car and drive home, crying and begging Kobe to forgive my inability to help him.

It is almost night before I hear him again, in the gentle wash of twilight that comes to cover the day and its brutal events. He is asking to talk with me, and though I am once more unwilling to face him, I slip out alone to a quiet spot and wait for him. I sense him here in my secluded spot, a bouncy puppy again, just on the edge of where my eyes can see into the gathering dusk.

"Kobe, I am so sorry," I begin.

But he stops me.

"I'm sorry, Mom. I didn't think I could do what I wanted in the body I was in. I was ready to leave it and I was so impatient. When I got sick, I took the chance and let it be. Then I saw how sad you were, how much it hurt you, and I tried to fight it, but I couldn't. I didn't think about you, or my sister, Trinket."

It will be days before I can grasp what he is telling me. It will be days before I can allow for

the possibility of his soul's plan in all that has
happened on this day. But as I listen to him, as
I commune with my little puppy in soul form, I
begin to let go of my guilt. I allow room for Kobe
and me to complete our life together. I allow
space for us to reconnect.

Sudden
Quickly, without time to prepare or fully
understand.

We have time to accept the coming transition
when our animal companions are at the end of
a long life or facing a terminal illness. We have time to
grow accustomed to the thought of living without them
in the forms we recognize and love. We have a transitional
period before their transition. In a sudden transition, we
often have little or no warning that our animal companion will transition and we have little or no time to
prepare. The word "sudden" describes something that
happens without warning, something that occurs
seemingly without any transition from the previous state.
A sudden occurrence is often unexpected and abrupt.
In a sudden transition, the texture of our lives is changed
in an instant, and we have no time to prepare ourselves
for it.

We are deluged with emotions when our animals
transition, whether their transition is sudden or not.

But the emotional experience of a sudden transition can be far more intense and varied. We may experience panic, fear, anger, guilt, and sadness in overwhelming doses—so much so that we can be physically affected by it. We may feel that we can neither think nor breathe. We may feel numb and as if nothing happening around us is real. And we may bounce back and forth between all these emotional states in the space of a few moments, only to start the roller coaster over again in the next moment. We may berate ourselves for handling the crises in a manner we feel is wrong. We may berate ourselves for not being strong enough or wise enough or whatever our own particular "enough" is.

The sudden transition of our animal companions will bring out the human in us. Not the best or the worst, but simply the human. Coming face-to-face with the sudden transition of our beloved animal and the depth of our emotions can be not only more than we want to face, but much more than we feel we *can* face.

How can we achieve a conscious transition when we are in emotional shock, when we feel we have no time to even think, much less reach out and communicate with our cherished animal companions? How can we achieve a conscious transition when we are flooded with emotions like guilt, anger, and fear? Do we acknowledge the promise to our companions as they are being intubated? Do we celebrate our lives together as we are speeding to the emergency clinic? Do we try to become complete with our animal companions in the seconds before the veterinarian tells us it's too late? The answer is no, and surprisingly also yes.

Communication with your animal companion takes many forms. Sometimes you may talk with them or send them mental pictures to convey your message. But often the most profound communication happens in moments of silence, when you are just being with your companion, experiencing the bond you share. This is the most elemental and visceral level of communication one soul uses to connect with another, and it is not dependent on time or your ability to think clearly. You may or may not have time to reach out and talk with your animal in a sudden transition, but you can be sure that whatever you want and need to convey to your cherished friend will be easily transmitted on this elemental communication level.

The first step in achieving a conscious sudden transition is to remember this fundamental level of communication and know that you *will* reach your animal no matter what is happening or what emotions you are experiencing. Even if you feel you are blocked from communicating with your companion, you will not be. If all you can do is feel how much you love your friend, it will be enough.

There are three additional steps you can take to aid you in being present with and for your animal companion in a sudden transition. While these three steps may seem difficult at first, they are actually very simple.

Both humans and animals are emotional beings. Our emotions allow us to connect with each other and experience what it is to love. We humans tend to value rational thought over emotions, but without our feelings, our experiences of life through emotions, would we even know we were alive? Often, we seek to pick and choose our emotions, allowing only the "good" ones or the "strong" ones. But we rarely—if ever—get the desired result from repressing our emotions. Repressed emotions will invariably seep out into our lives, often causing physical illness and sometimes leaving us to deal with deeper and stronger versions of the originally repressed emotion. When we are dealing with emotions surrounding the sudden transition of a loved one, human or animal, we are more likely to want to repress our emotions than at other times, and we are more likely to face lasting repercussions if we do repress them.

I am the youngest of four children in my human family. I have two brothers who are much older than me. They each married and had baby boys while I was still in early grade school. Because my brothers and their new families chose to live close to our parents, my nephews were like siblings to me. We argued and fought together, picked on each other, defended each other, and listened to each other like siblings. I loved them very much (and still do).

When my first nephew was sixteen, he drowned in a canoeing accident. This was my first real experience with the transition of a loved one and I was caught so unaware by it that I didn't even think to repress my emotions of grief and loss. When my second nephew was twenty-three, he transitioned quickly and violently in a sawmill accident. This time I knew how losing the physical presence of someone you love dearly felt, and I did not want to feel those emotions. I chose instead to become angry and to stay angry. The cost of repressing my grief, turning my natural pain into anger, was severe depression. It was not until I allowed myself to feel all the emotions of this unwelcome and sudden loss that I was able to climb out of my depression. Only then could I become complete with my nephew and his transition.

When your animal companion transitions from age or a long illness, you will have time to come to terms with your emotions. When your companion transitions suddenly, it may feel like everything is happening at once and that you cannot think past the surge of emotions that grip and tear at you.

The second step in a conscious sudden transition is to allow your emotions to be without judgment. If you are feeling anger—whether that anger is aimed at yourself, another human, or your animal companion— just allow the anger to be. If you are feeling guilt or remorse, allow it to be. If you are frightened or anguished or hysterical or even numb, just allow those emotions to be. Your emotions are not right or wrong, they simply *are.* Any attempt to control or rule your emotions, to allow only the "good" emotions, may leave you unable to focus on anything but the unwanted emotions.

Instead, acknowledge any emotions you may feel. If you are feeling panicked, do not try to fight your panic or add to your distress by thinking your emotion of panic is wrong. When you resist an emotion, you are only feeding it as your mind struggles to help you understand what is true for you. Notice your emotion of panic. Tell yourself, "I am feeling panicked now. I don't know if I should, but I do." Allow your panic, anger, guilt, and any other emotion you may feel to just be. Observe what you are feeling without judging or condemning yourself for something you cannot control.

You can even talk with your animal companion about your emotions. In any form of communication, it is the soul of the other being we are communicating with. Whether your animal is conscious or unconscious, you can still talk with them. If you are angry that your dog escaped and was hit by a car, tell your dog! The soul of your companion will know that your anger comes from your love and will not last. If you are angry with yourself for leaving the gate open, tell your dog that too. The soul that is your animal companion will not judge your actions and will not judge how you are feeling. Your companion will give you space to feel all your emotions. You may have only moments, but talking with your animal companion on the elemental level of communication about the emotions his or her sudden transition is creating for you can happen in an instant.

Allowing your emotions to be, giving yourself space to feel whatever you are feeling without judging either yourself or your emotions, will give you room to proceed regardless of your emotional state. When you allow your emotions to be whatever they may be, you will free yourself to create and hold the space of love and peace for your animal to transition.

The third step in a conscious sudden transition is to let go of how things are or were supposed to be. When you brought your animal companion into your life, you may have had visions of how they would spend their last days in their current body. If your animal is young, you may have had plans for all of the adventures and everyday life you and your companion would experience together. A sudden transition eliminates all options but the one in front of you.

We live in a world created by choice, both our own choices and the choices of others. This can be a frightening concept when the choices of others conflict with our own choices, either for ourselves or for others. Seeking control of our world and those in it is a natural part of the survival instinct. As natural as this may be, it is also almost impossible to control anything beyond our own actions and reactions.

This need to protect ourselves is often strongest when it is centered on the loved ones in our lives, particularly in regards to the circumstances of their transition. We consider it painful but acceptable for our animal companions to transition when they are elderly, but not when they are young. We consider it equally unacceptable for our elderly companions to transition through an accident or an unexpected, quick illness.

When our companions transition suddenly, we not only lose them physically, we also lose the dreams we had for their lives with us. Without warning, we are thrust into a situation that is not of our choosing and which we can neither change nor control. To be present for our animals, to allow space for a conscious transition, we must let go of our visions and allow room for what is to be.

How do we let go of our dreams for our animal companion? How do we reconcile what we had hoped would happen with an undesirable and possibly brutal reality? Once again, we simply let it be.

Acknowledge that whatever circumstances led to your companion's sudden transition are not what you wanted or hoped for. Acknowledge the plans and dreams you had for and with your companion. Allow yourself to grieve for these lost plans and dreams. Then acknowledge the circumstances of your animal's transition without judgment. Be in the moment with your companion.

Just as it is important to acknowledge and accept your emotions, it is important to acknowledge and accept your need to control the circumstances of your animal's transition. Accept both your desire to change what is happening and what is actually happening.

As you let go of how you expected your animal companion to live or transition, you will give yourself permission to let your animal companion transition. You will allow room to say whatever there is for you to say to your animal. You will find the time, no matter how little you may have, to give your animal permission to transition. You will create a space in which you and your animal may celebrate and complete your life together, even if you only have moments. You will allow room to be fully present with and for your companion in *this* moment, the moment of what is.

The fourth step in a conscious sudden transition is to allow room for both your need to understand why and the knowledge that you may not have an answer for the why before your animal companion transitions—or even while you are in this life. We humans have a need to understand the reasons behind what happens in our lives, whether what happens is perceived as good or bad. We believe that when we understand why, we can make the good things happen again and prevent the bad things from reoccurring. This is one of the ways we attempt to control our world and our experience of our world.

When your animal is transitioning suddenly, it is normal to ask why, to wonder what you could have done differently or what you missed. It is impossible not to have these questions, not to feel the need to understand why this is happening.

Many circumstances can lead to the sudden transition of an animal. They may eat something they shouldn't have eaten. They may be hit by a car or severely injured by an animal or a person. Dogs can transition rapidly from bloat, cats from cardiomyopathy, and horses from aneurysms. The list of circumstances that can cause a sudden transition is long. As animal guardians, keeping our animal companions safe from every circumstance that can cause a sudden transition may seem like an almost impossible task. And yet we persevere, consciously and unconsciously watching over our animal companions, accepting every day they remain in their current body as the reward for our vigilance.

Sometimes, no matter how vigilant we are, our animals transition suddenly. There are many places where we cannot or choose not to take our companions and because of that, they sometimes transition when they are not with us. We may let down our guard, not know how dangerous something is, or otherwise have a momentary lapse in our constant vigil. Sometimes our animals have some underlying and undetected health issue that causes them to transition suddenly.

The emotion of guilt can become overwhelming when our companions transition suddenly. Whether our animals were old or young, whether the circumstances of their transitioning were unpredictable or easily avoidable, we can become paralyzed with guilt over our real or perceived action or lack of action. We can become obsessed with the need to protect ourselves and the souls we love from ever experiencing this again.

In asking the question why, we are seeking either confirmation of or absolution from our guilt. We are looking for a way to promise ourselves and our animals that whatever this circumstance is, we will never let it happen again.

Embrace your need to know why your animal companion is transitioning suddenly and allow yourself space to understand what is happening so you can learn from it. There may well be valuable lessons for you. At the same time, give yourself permission to set aside your questions for the moment and be present with your animal companion. Give yourself permission to set aside any guilt you may feel. The answer to why your animal is transitioning is not as important as being with your animal as he or she transitions. You will have time to ask why later. Let yourself be with your companion now.

And I invite you to consider and play with the notion that the answer to why your animal companion is transitioning suddenly may be as simple as this: he or she chose to. Consider this possibility. We each chose to come into this life, animal and human alike. We chose how, when, and where we would enter this plane of existence. It is also possible that we chose how, when, and where we would exit this plane of existence—how, when, and where we would transition from life to life.

This level of choice does not negate our promise to hold each life sacred. It does not negate our promise to take care of the souls we love, to watch over and guard them to the best of our ability. It only serves to remind us that we are each here to learn, experience, and remember. It only serves to remind us that when our animals transition they are not ending, they are only moving on to continue their journey of learning, experiencing, and remembering.

Creating a conscious transition with your animal companion in a sudden transition may at best seem challenging and at worst seem impossible. But when you allow you and your animal room to be who and what you each are in the moment, when you give yourself room to feel your emotions and, for the moment, let go of the hows and the whys, you will create a space of love and peace for your animal. Allow yourself to be, vulnerability and all. You cannot get this wrong, just love your animal companion and let him or her know you are there for them.

Chapter Eight Workbook Exercises

1. If you have experienced a sudden transition with one of your animal companions, take time to write about this experience. Make special note of the emotions this transition brought up for you. Examine any lingering emotions or blame you may have about this experience.

2. Write a letter to your transitioned animal companion. Tell them everything you wanted them to know but didn't have time to say. Let them know how their transition made you feel. Be honest without judgment about the emotions you experienced. Consider giving or asking for forgiveness or understanding if you have unresolved conflict about how your animal transitioned.

3. Write a letter to yourself from your transitioned animal companion. Allow yourself to simply write the first ideas that come to your mind. You can even structure the letter as a question and answer session between you and your transitioned companion. If you feel that what

you're writing or about to write couldn't have come from your animal companion, let yourself write it out anyway. This will help you to reach out to your animal and become complete with the sudden transition.

4. Give yourself permission to let go of any lingering guilt or anger over your animal's transition. Give yourself permission to move forward in your relationship with your transitioned companion.

CHAPTER NINE

Communicating with Your Animal Companion After the Transition

Andrea

Sony had flown from her body, Kobe ripped from his, you ... sifted ... from yours, like a long broken sigh before falling into sleep.

I remember holding your body as it cooled, rocking your body to comfort myself, but finding none.

Roxy

I hovered near you as you held my body, trying to reach through your grief, but it was too strong, too new, too raw. I would wait until your storm subsided, until you could hear me again.

Andrea

I felt so alone on that ride home. I could never be alone when you were with me, but now I couldn't feel you, either physically or spiritually. I was adrift, drowning in my grief. When Liz lost her old companion, Chino, a few years before, she'd seen him at home, from the corner of her eye, in his favorite resting places. I walked through the door looking for you, but I saw nothing.

Roxy

I was there, and I was also not there. In the hours after a transition, there is much to be done. I was rejuvenated by my complete connection to Source, and I wanted to talk with you, to tell you exactly how I was. I was free, I was happy, and yet I too was alone, waiting for a break in the fog of your pain. It wasn't our plan for me to come back in my Roxy body. You would need to listen carefully, for now we would connect fully on the soul level.

Andrea

Gradually, I began to feel our connection again. Sometimes I felt nothing and sometimes I heard your voice in my mind as clear as before you left. I remember driving to work the day I picked up your ashes. It was harder than I thought to bring them home, and I was trying not to cry before work.

"It's all right to feel this, let it be," you said, breaking through my meditation. "Humans need a focal *point. When you write, light a candle and know that I'm there, writing with you."*

I was bemused. I understood your message, but couldn't understand your reference to my writing. I filed it away for the time, but it came back to me that weekend when my grief threatened to overwhelm me. I turned to writing as a way to process the feelings I couldn't control. At first, I wrote only poems. I had no destination, I only wanted to put on paper how I felt, to see it clearly, to capture it and in so doing, to understand and accept it.

Roxy

Yes! You were listening. I was getting through, and now our healing and our future could begin. You wanted to see me, to connect with me in a spectacular, undeniable way. But that was not our plan. However, I did have something for you, something quiet but powerful. Would you be aware enough to catch it?

Andrea

I heard your message; you were here. I only had to open my mind's eye to you and feel the connection to my soul companion.

As I wrote, I began to see the words to capture not my loss, but what you are to me, the gift we share.

I bought a candle that weekend, randomly grabbing the first white candle on the shelf, and set it beside your ashes on my computer desk. I lit it that night and started to put us on paper. And you were there, writing with me. We wrote into the night, only stopping when exhaustion claimed my body. I rose and blew out the candle, catching a whiff of its fragrance in the gently curling smoke. It was vanilla. I had sat with you so many times, hugging you to me and calling you my beautiful vanilla-face girl. Your plush face was the color of vanilla cookies, your nose the color of a vanilla bean. I laughed and I cried, sad that I couldn't hold my beautiful vanilla-faced puppy again, and overjoyed by this undeniable gift of connection you had given me.

Roxy

There were tears in your eyes that night, but they were the tears of healing. You had caught my quiet message, my singular way to show myself to you from a remembered physical connection. We could both heal now, and move forward together.

Energy

The spark that animates us, the part of us that
is connected with the Universe.

"Are you your body, or do you have your body? Are
you your brain, or do you have your brain?"

The doctor's words were clear, and I understood his
questions. I even knew my answers, but I could not
seem to form the words. My thoughts were muddled
and confused. My emotions swung wildly from panic
to anger to crushing sadness, and I could not corral
them. I could not catch my breath and find respite from
the emotional storm that flooded over me. I held back
tears and tried to answer the questions in the simple,
direct way I could have just a week earlier. I fought to
calm the emotional deluge in my brain and to remember the correct words to answer his questions.

The doctor repeated his questions. "Are you your
brain, or do you have your brain? Think about this. Your
answer will determine the best path to your recovery."

And then, halting, stumbling through words as I
worked to make the connection between my thoughts
and my speech, I answered, "I am not my brain. I am
not my body. I am still here, though I don't understand
or recognize how my brain is responding."

I began writing this chapter on reconnecting with
our transitioned animal companions on October 27,
2011. I worked for hours, putting together the words to

say that the most important part of us, our energy, our soul, does not die when the body stops working, that we go on beyond our body's death. In the late afternoon, I took a break from my work for a quick trip to the grocery store. I was not the same when I returned.

On my way to the grocery store, my small car was rear-ended by a large SUV. I was stopped and the SUV was going at a speed of 40 to 50 mph when it hit me. The next thing I clearly remember was the other driver knocking on my widow, asking if I could move. I did not break any bones; I did not have any cuts. My body did not look injured, but my brain had slammed into the uneven and rough interior of both the back and front of my skull. At the time I only knew that I had lost my peripheral vision, that I was not steady on my feet, and that I felt as if my thoughts were wandering in a deep and murky fog. Later I would learn that my injury was called a TBI, or traumatic brain injury. Very soon I would understand that everything I knew and understood about my ability to communicate, to interact with others, and to function emotionally in life was damaged and no longer worked in ways familiar to me. I was still in there, but it was like living in an interactive suit that no longer functioned in ways I could understand or recognize.

Months later, it is still a challenge to write, even though I have come a long way on my journey of healing. It was once easy to put my thoughts into words; now it is a frustrating process. My hands do not connect as well with my brain and what I actually write is often not quite what I intended. But my ideas are still the same! What I have learned and remembered in this life's journey is still very clear, but expressing it takes more effort. I look back at what I wrote on October 27, 2011, and I can no longer remember where I was going with it or what I was trying to say. And I no longer need to.

I know that I was writing about how we view life after death. I know that I wanted to talk about the lack of proof for either life after death or no life after death. I wanted to talk about the possibility of energy transferring from corporeal to noncorporeal.

Now I see that proof or theories carry little weight. They are interesting, thought provoking, and entertaining, but cannot carry the day. It is for you to search your soul and determine what resonates with you, what rings true.

Dealing with a traumatic brain injury has not been easy. It has been one of the most difficult things I have experienced, and yet, it has also come with gifts.

I am so very clear that we reside in and around our bodies, that we use them to interact with our world and those around us, but that we are not our bodies. I have sat back within my body and watched my brain respond in ways that bewilder me, that I know are not me. My body and my brain are expressions of me. They allow me to interact with and experience this world and the other souls in it. They give me a way to define who and what I am while I am here, and my soul harmonizes with them. I celebrate my body. I celebrate my brain, even with the brain injury. But I am not this physical form, however complex it may be. I am so much more than chemical reactions and firing neurons. I am a being residing in this amazing biological suit. And when this biological suit has finished its mission, I will continue.

So it is with our beloved animal companions. They each have biological suits that allow them to interact with all around them, and they continue when the suit's time is finished.

We would not question whether we would still be able to communicate with someone after they changed clothes or moved to a different state. Why would we question whether we can communicate with a soul that has shed his or her biological suit and moved to the state of energy?

We don't question our ability to communicate by telephone with a family member or friend who is not with us, though we cannot see them and have only the familiar sound of their voice, their speech patterns, and their personality to prove that we have reached them. Why then would we question the familiar feel of our animal companion's soul, the resonance of their unique being, when we communicate with their transitioned soul? It is all the same.

I do believe that our science will eventually catch up and give us a concrete explanation for this communication. Galileo once said, "All truths are easy to understand once they are discovered; the point is to discover them." I believe this applies to the concept of life after transitions and our ability to communicate with souls that have transitioned from life to life. But we do not have to wait for that concrete explanation. We have only to listen beyond the senses our biological suit offers us, for we are all far more than the physical.

Communicating with your transitioned animal companion can be both a very simple matter and a very difficult matter. This communication is simple because your connection with your animal companion is never broken. You can reach out and talk with your animal friend just as you did before. The soul that is your friend is wholly intact, and you will communicate with that soul in the same manner you did prior to his or her transition.

This communication is difficult because you may cloud your connection to your animal companion with preconditioned beliefs about transition being an ending or a death. You may also cloud your connection with worries about your ability to reach your animal companion, and you may cloud it further with your grief.

I had only just begun to build my inter-species communication muscles when Roxy transitioned. Roxy was a beautiful silver cocker spaniel, and she is the soul who guided me as I learned to truly see the universe around me with all the wonder and beauty it holds. She patiently waited for me to recognize our connection and firmly guided me to see that she was more than a pretty dog body, she was an amazing and loving soul inhabiting a pretty dog body. Roxy was and is very special to me, and I was devastated when she left her body.

I had successfully communicated with several animals before Roxy left her dog body, including my revealing talk with Kobe after his transition. But Roxy's unexpected transition left me overwhelmed with doubts and grief that grew until I could not see beyond them. I felt so alone without the physical presence of my companion and guide. It was as if I had been picking my way through a complex maze in a well lit room when the lights suddenly went out. As much as I wanted to connect with Roxy on my own, I thought about asking my animal communication mentor to speak with her for me. I would eventually have done that, but then Roxy broke through the haze of my doubt and grief to reach me on her own.

Her process of breaking through my self-imposed walls was slow and subtle. I had been looking for grand gestures. I had wanted to physically see and hear her. But her methods were more finely tuned to our unique relationship.

Roxy left her body the day after Christmas in 2003. The following day I sat in the gloom of an early and cloudy winter morning, missing her as I would miss my own breath if it stopped. As I sat there, wrapped in my grief, I began to feel a separate grief flow through me. The resonance of this new grief was not my own, but it carried a hint of the familiar. I let this grief wash over me, mentally sampling its taste and texture until I began to understand that it was coming from Roxy. I could not reach out and talk with her yet, but she was sending something of herself through to me—her own sorrow. I knew that she had been ready to leave her body and could no longer stay in it. But before that moment, I had not understood her sorrow in having lost our physical connection.

Several days later I was driving to work when a song on the radio broke through my concentration. The song was perfect for my mood, the grief I was processing, and it almost seemed to be a direct message from Roxy. As more days and more drives to work went by, many more songs jumped out to catch my attention with the same intensity as the first. Soon I could neither ignore their messages nor the fact that they were Roxy's way of reaching me.

My first real communication with Roxy came on the day I picked up her ashes. I held the small round urn for what seemed like hours, bewildered by how her once vibrant body was now contained in such an insignificant and silent vessel. I needed to be at work soon, and I struggled not to cry. I did not want to give in to the grief I knew could wash over me at the smallest break in my defenses. My thoughts were abruptly interrupted by a familiar and compelling "voice" in my mind.

"It's all right to feel this. Let it be."

With that one sentence and the resonance of Roxy's thought pattern ringing in my soul, my self-imposed blocks crumbled and our communication was restored. I let go of my tight control and my fears; I let both the grief and the relief wash over me.

Roxy had broken through my barriers of doubt and grief, and there would be no turning back.

Even when we can see and hold our animal companions, communication can seem complicated or even impossible. When they have moved out of the body we know, it can seem as if we have no solid ground to stand on, no tangible thing that we can hold on to and use as a guide. It can seem as if we are truly grasping at thin air as we attempt to communicate using only our energy, our soul.

In my experience as an animal communicator, I have never run across a transitioned animal companion who was not trying to talk with his or her humans, who did not have a message, even if it was only, "Thank you." If your animal companion has transitioned, and you are struggling to feel her or his presence, to communicate and connect as you did before, first know that your animal friend is also trying to reach you. And it may be that your struggles are making the process harder. Acknowledge your fears, doubts, and any guilt you may feel. The more you fight these emotions, the more life you give them. Let them have room to just be. Then examine your emotions, giving them and yourself enough space so you can begin to understand why you're having them at this time. As you give yourself space to feel your emotions, whatever they may be, you will be cutting off the frantic fuel on which they survive.

Doubt and fear are part of the human experience and more often than not, these emotions have little to do with our actual abilities in any given area. If you wonder whether or not you can communicate with your transitioned animal, you may also fear that you will be unable to connect if you try. You may avoid trying to communicate because you believe there will be great pain in trying and failing. And you may worry that if you do try to connect with your transitioned animal and are unable to do so, it will change how you perceive the relationship you shared with your companion. You may worry what trying and failing to communicate will mean about you and your animal friend. But as long as you stay in the safe zone of not knowing, you will miss the opportunity to connect with your transitioned animal and the joy of doing so.

Embrace your doubts; delve into your fears. You cannot resolve these strong emotions if you fight against them. Explore what you think it would mean about you and your relationship with your animal friend if you could not connect with them. When you face these worries and fears head-on, they are likely to lose their power. You will see your fears on their most basic level: They are simply stories you are telling yourself. Let go of your fears; tell yourself a new story.

Even if it takes days or weeks before you can connect with your transitioned animal companion—either personally or with the help of a professional animal communicator—know that the amount of time it takes to connect says nothing about your relationship with your friend. What matters is that you faced your doubts and made the connection. However long it takes and however it happens, know that it is okay.

The emotion of guilt is another insidious and powerful block to communication with our transitioned companions. We may wonder if we did all we could for our animal friends and if our actions were truly what they wanted. Did we do enough? Did we let our animal companions suffer too long? Did we make our friends leave their bodies before they were ready? When we feel this guilt over how we handled the transition, we can fear connecting with our transitioned animals as much as we look forward to it. What will they say to us? Will they be harsh or critical of our actions? If so, how will that affect us and our memories? We may even feel that we have no right to reach out to them because we fear we have let them down in the most important moment of their life with us and worry that they will not forgive us.

Just like doubts and fears, feelings of guilt will dissolve only when you embrace them. Examine your guilt. Review the choices you made and the actions you took in regards to your animal companion's transition. Imagine all of your worst-case scenarios about what your animal will say to you about the transition. Explore what you are making these imagined conversations mean. And then let it all go.

Whatever the circumstances of your animal companion's transition are, there may well be a purpose behind them. Your animal companion may have chosen those exact circumstances, and you may have chosen them as well. Give yourself room to learn from this experience. And listen with an open heart for your transitioned animal's communication. The soul of your companion will literally see the circumstances of their transitioning from a new perspective now that they have transitioned. It is most likely that you have done nothing to feel guilty over, and your transitioned animal will put your heart at ease with his or her thoughts. If you *did* make choices and take actions that were not in keeping with your highest nature, your transitioned animal companion can be a loving teacher for you as you learn whatever there is for you to learn in this experience.

Grief can sometimes be the most difficult block of all. It is not possible to lose the physical form of your dear companion and not feel sorrow. When we grieve, we mourn for what we have lost. Even though our animal companions do not cease to exist, even though all that is core to their beings continue, we still experience loss. We lose the physicality of our companions, the ability to look into their eyes, laugh at their play, and snuggle with them. We lose the ability to reach out and touch them. And no matter how much we understand that our animal companions have transitioned out of their bodies, this loss of the physical connection is tangible and powerful.

In our grief, our thoughts linger on how our companion was before the transition and the nature of the relationship we had with them when they were corporeal. As we grieve, we look back at what we have lost, and it can be almost impossible to look forward. This part of grieving is natural, and we cannot and should not try to bypass it. It is too important for our healing. But as we look back, we can also make room to look forward, to mentally clear the way for a new connection and relationship with the souls of our animal companions.

When your animal companion transitions, allow yourself to grieve this very real loss, find ways to honor the relationship you and your companion shared, and take the time you need to find healing for your pain. And in remembering how your dear friend was before, take time to be aware of how your animal may be reaching out to you now.

As you let go of your emotions, as doubt, fear, sorrow and guilt run their course, also let go of any speculation about how you and your animal companion will communicate now that he or she has transitioned.

I had many expectations of how Roxy would make her presence known after her transition. If I had been able to "see" Kobe out of the corner of my eye, surely I would have no trouble seeing Roxy. After all, she was my teacher, the companion of my soul. I came home from the emergency clinic where she left her body, drowning in grief and expecting to see her sitting in her favorite chair, waiting to welcome me home and tell me the answers to all of my questions. I was crushed and frightened when I didn't see her. I looked for her everywhere in the way I expected to see her, and my fear and doubt grew with every moment I could not find her. Had I been wrong all along? Maybe I had never really talked with her or any of the others. Worse yet, maybe *she* had nothing to say to me. Maybe she did not want to communicate with me! The more I clung to my vision of how our communication should look, the more I fed the emotional blocks to the communication I so desired.

As with your emotions, acknowledge your expectations and let them go. You and your animal companion may communicate in exactly the way you imagine, or it may be something altogether different, and perhaps even more wonderful than what you imagined. Let yourself be open. Listen for any of the ways your animal friend may reach out to you. It may be songs, which is how Roxy reached out to me. It may be smells or sounds. It may be thoughts that do not feel like you own. And the communication may even come through memories. There are hundreds of ways your animal may reach out to you. Give you and your animal friend room to find the communication that will best suit *your* unique relationship.

Sometimes we reconnect with our transitioned animal companions in ways we never dreamed of and just when we think we may never talk with them again.

Several months ago I had the privilege to facilitate communication between Sam and his dog, Apples. Apples had been diagnosed with autoimmune hemolytic anemia disease many years before her transition. Autoimmune hemolytic anemia is a brutal disease that is hard to catch early on and often kills its victims within days—if not hours—of diagnosis. The illness had been caught early. Aggressive immediate treatment and rigorous daily maintenance treatments had managed to give Apples ten more years of joy, love, and life.

In the fall of 2011, Apples was diagnosed with an inoperable tumor in her abdomen. When Sam and his wife Laura first noticed Apples' declining health, they assumed her autoimmune hemolytic anemia had grown worse and they would need to step up her daily treatments. They never expected to hear that she had a tumor in her abdomen, growing into a vein. They began palliative treatment for Apples, hoping against hope to reduce the tumor and at the very least give Apples relief from her new pain.

Sam called me shortly after the diagnosis and asked me to talk with Apples for them. He wanted to know if Apples wanted the treatments and how she felt, both physically and mentally. I connected with Apples and was overwhelmed with the love I felt flowing from her for Sam and Laura. "They are everything to me," Apples told me. "I have never felt such love before. Even when I don't feel well, I am so happy to be with them!" Apples went on to tell me that she didn't want to leave her body but she didn't know how long she could hold on. "It's getting harder to stay in this body, but I want to stay! Please let my people know that I will try my best to stay longer and I will take any medicine they give me. I trust them."

Sam and Laura were encouraged by her words. They continued to do everything they could for Apples and researched other possible treatments. Despite all of their efforts, Apples became worse. One morning they awoke to find Apples listless and unable to eat. They both knew the time had come to give Apples peace and true relief from her growing pain. They took her to the vet that same morning and held her close as the vet injected the drug that would release her from her body.

A few days later, Sam called me again. Though Laura had done more of the day-to-day care for Apples, Sam and Apples had a special connection and Sam hoped to communicate with her transitioned soul. He had tried on his own but could not get through to her. He was concerned that his choice to euthanize her might have upset her, and he worried that he had let her down, had not honored her wish to stay in her body for as long as she could.

Even before I reached out to Apples, I felt her presence. She sent me a mental picture of Sam enclosed in a bubble of his guilt and grief. She was running around the bubble, charging it and body slamming it, trying anything she could to break through and connect with Sam. "I'm not angry!" She yelled in my mind. "I'm so thankful they gave me so long in my body with them. I don't think anyone else would have done more for me, given me so much time, so much love."

I gave Sam Apples' message and asked him to let go of his guilt and make peace with his worries. I let him know that Apples was waiting on him; he did not have to wait for her.

A week later, I heard from Sam again, and the news he shared with me left me smiling for days. Sam had spent a lot of time thinking about Apples' message and finding a way to let go of his emotions of guilt. Finally, late one night, he talked aloud to Apples and asked her to please let him know that she was there, waiting for him. He went to bed, hoping that Apples would come to him in a dream. He awoke hours later, not having dreamed of Apples and unable to fall back asleep. He wandered to his office in the basement of his home, not even bothering to turn on lights. The dark gloom seemed to suit his grief and despair. As he sat staring at his dark computer screen, he noticed a flashing light in the far corner of the basement.

"I thought at first that something was reflecting light from passing cars on the street," he told me. "But when I got closer, I realized that the window was too far away and the angle was wrong. Not to mention that there was not that much traffic at 3:00 AM! The light was beautiful, flashing white with occasional bursts of color. When I reached the corner, I could see that the light was coming from an unused solar panel I'd stored in the basement. The more I watched that light, the more I felt I recognized it somehow. After a minute, I got it. This was Apples! I always thought of her as so full of life and light. This was Apples' way of letting me know she was waiting for me!"

I could hear the wonder in Sam's voice as he spoke. I could almost feel his elation and relief at having bridged the gap between himself and his special little girl. And I could feel Apples' joy and contentment at having broken through the bubble of Sam's grief and guilt, her delight over connecting with her special person.

Connecting with your animal companion after his or her transition may happen with little effort in a moment. But it may take time to work through your emotional barriers. Your animal companion may make her or his presence known in a spectacular way, or in a subtle reminder of your life together. You may seek help from a professional animal communicator, or you may make the connection with your animal on your own. However this communication happens, it will be beautiful. It will be a continuation of the unique relationship of the being that is you, who lives in but is not your biological suit, with the being that is your companion, who lived in an animal suit.

Chapter Nine Workbook Exercises

1. If your animal companion has transitioned and you feel unable to communicate with him or her, take a moment and write down how this makes you feel. What blocks may be in the way of your communication?

2. Next, take out a piece of paper and write down what your feelings and the blocks you discovered to communicating with your animal mean about you, your animal companion, and the relationship you share. Be honest and bold in your assessment of the meaning you are giving to your difficulty in reaching your animal. Do not judge this meaning, but be thorough.

3. When you have completed writing out the meaning you are assigning to your communication blocks, review your list and write the following beside each item: This is not the truth. This is just a story I'm telling myself. Read it aloud several times until you know in the core of your being that all of the meaning you have assigned to communicating or not communicating with your transitioned animal companion is truly just a story you told yourself. When you are done, tear up the piece of paper and visualize letting go of the meaning you have given to these blocks.

4. Give yourself permission to communicate with your transitioned animal companion in any form that works for the two of you. Be open and aware to how your animal may be reaching out to you.

CHAPTER TEN

Taking Care of Yourself After the Transition

Arden

It's late evening and the warm spring day has turned cold. The bold tulips blooming in the garden have closed their petals tight against the chilled air and are waiting for the next day's warmth to open and dance again beneath the sun's enticing light.

Jordan and I, along with our two dogs, Cruz and Capo, are curled up together on our couch. The four of us snuggle close on this cold spring evening. In their own way, they have each told me that they feel deep sorrow. I can feel their pain, almost as powerfully as I feel my own. We are all grieving the physical loss of Arden, who left her body this morning.

Just last night, we had been a family of five snuggling together, playing together, and cherishing those final hours with Arden in her body.

Now, even though we know that all that is truly Arden is still with us, her favorite spot by the fireplace is empty. Her soft bed of plush blankets, placed with care by our bed so that we could watch over her through the night, will not be warmed by her small and vibrant body again.

Arden used every ounce of that body to express her vivacious and youthful soul. She never held back anything, and even at age fourteen—blind, deaf, and dealing with a third round of cancer—she still ran to greet us, even though she occasionally ran into a wall and not our arms. She still expressed her happiness with full-body wags and enthusiastic panting, still expressed her displeasure to Cruz and Capo with loud growls and ferocious, if often inaccurate, snaps.

Arden's soul and her vivacious spirit are not diminished by her transition from her body. I have only to think that I miss her and I see her grinning furry face in my mind's eye. She says to me, "How can you miss me? I'm still here!"

Jordan has experienced this too, and we are both delighted by this quick and definitive connection with Arden's transitioned soul. My soul is thrilled to know that Arden is still with us, that communicating with her is less than a thought away.

But my hands ... my hands ache to pull Arden close and touch her silky ears. My lips ache to press a kiss on her velvet-soft and cinnamon colored face. My ears long to hear her bird-like chirps of joy at dinnertime, the steady sound of her breathing, and the gentle snuffles of her soft kisses on my cheek.

I burrow deeper into our cocoon of four, thinking that Jordan's hands must ache just as mine do, that Capo and Cruz must miss the familiar scent of their companion, the warmth of her body snuggled against theirs during a doggie nap.

We are all feeling the keen-edged loss of Arden's physical form and we offer to each other the comfort and reassurance of each other's physical presence. We curl together against the cold of our grief and wait for the next day's light.

Grief

The painful emotional and sometime physical response to the loss of a loved one.

We humans are, for the most part, uncomfortable with grief on a profound level. Out of this discomfort we often create rules and expectations of how we and others should grieve. For some, grief "should" leave you shattered and unable to cope. For others, grief is to be suppressed and you "should" carry on with dignity and courage.

I cannot tell you how I learned my rules of grief. No one ever sat me down and said, "This is how you should feel and behave when you experience the loss of a loved one." And still I developed my own ideas of what was expected of me when facing loss. I wasn't even aware of these rules until my nephew drowned and I began to express my loss in what I felt would be an acceptable manner.

These unwritten and often unspoken rules of grief can be as varied as the cultures and individuals that make up the human race. But for many, if not most, there is one common element, the element of expectation. Whatever rules we follow in grief, we may do so because we want to, consciously or unconsciously, live up to what we believe is expected of us.

In my rules, grief is to be faced with quiet courage. I am expected to think of others and be strong for them. It's all right for me to cry, but not break down and sob. I should not make a scene but if I do, it should be brief and never be repeated.

I was introduced to the concept of grief stages in the weeks after my nephew died. I took it to heart and began to examine my emotions to see if they fit into where I felt I was expected to be in the grief process. I wondered if I was moving through the stages correctly and if I would achieve closure with his death in the appropriate time frame. Even as I grieved, I added to my list of rules and worked to live up to the new expectations that came with them.

The rules and expectations we humans develop for grief are neither right nor wrong. They are simply our attempt to cope with the pain of losing someone we love. They are, in some ways, an attempt to establish control over an uncontrollable situation. For some people, the grief rules and expectations they have learned can serve as a source of comfort. For others, the rules and expectations can hinder their journey of healing through grief.

I invite you to examine any preconditioned rules or expectations you may have around grieving. Do these rules serve you or do they hinder you? Grief is an individual and personal thing. Allow yourself to grieve in the way you want, not in the way you feel is expected of you.

When our grief is over the loss of an animal companion, the rules and expectations can become especially murky. Some people will understand how deeply this loss can affect you, and others may not. Our friends and family may be supportive of our grief and some of them may not understand how you can hurt so much when it was "just an animal."

Should you grieve as much for the loss of your animal companion as you would for a human? How long and in what manner should you grieve for your animal? The answers to these questions are no different than if you had lost a human. You will grieve as much as you grieve, for as long as you grieve and in whatever manner you grieve. Your grief for any one loss cannot be compared

141

to another loss, whether it is an animal or a human. Grief is not objective, and it can be different each time we experience it. There is no scale or chart your grief needs to be defined by. And know that the loss of your beloved animal companion can be a very difficult loss, perhaps for you the most difficult loss you have experienced.

Our animals are the only ones who give us truly unconditional love. They never question our choice in clothing or careers; they do not care if we are skinny or fat. They love us when we are fun to be around and when we are sad or mad or scared. They see past every external condition and love the beings that we are. How can we not be devastated by the physical loss of the beings that see us exactly as we are and not only love us through it all, but also express their love with no reservation?

In the weeks after Roxy left her body, I struggled to find a balance between grieving and being productive at work each day. I had lost the physical presence of the soul who saw me for who I was and loved me for all of it. I wanted nothing more than to curl up on the couch and not move but that wasn't an option. So I fluctuated between putting on a brave face at work and allowing myself to grieve when I left for the day.

One evening I stopped at the grocery store before going home. I was sad but calm at the start of my grocery shopping trip and more focused on what I needed to buy than my grief—until I reached for a box of my favorite cereal. When I picked up that cereal, I thought of how Roxy had sat quietly beside me each morning while I ate. I always gave her the last little bit of my cereal. It was one of our daily rituals, a simple and small thing. The memory of it came to me so fast and was so vivid that I began to sob right there in the cereal aisle. I was embarrassed and ashamed. I was crying in public. My rules did not allow that and worse yet, people were looking at me, witnessing my lack of strength.

One woman actually approached me and asked if I was all right. In that moment, I had a choice. I could continue living by my rules of grief or I could just grieve. I told her that I was physically fine but my dog had died a few weeks earlier and I was very sad. That wonderful stranger did not lecture me on being strong or even say, "It was just a dog." She expressed her very real condolences and offered to get a tissue for me. On the drive home I thought about my cereal aisle tears and her reaction. I realized it wouldn't have mattered if she hadn't understood. I was grieving the physical loss of a soul that felt like another part of me. If that loss made me cry in the grocery store or anywhere else, then that was an appropriate reaction for *me*. This loss, this grief, was my journey and no one else's. Only I could choose how and when to grieve.

I would like to say the grocery store incident was the defining moment in my quest to grieve without rules, but the ingrained habits and beliefs of a lifetime usually do not disappear with one choice. More often, it takes a series of choices, a series of defining moments. I faced that same choice many times as I grieved for Roxy, Arden, EddieMac. Sometimes I made the choice to just allow my grief to be and sometimes I chose to give in to my rules. Along the way, I have realized that the beauty of healing, of learning and remembering, is not that you make the right choice, but just that you see there *is* a choice.

As often as you can, make the choice to feel all of the emotions the physical loss of your animal companion will create in you. Even if you have already connected with the transitioned soul of your companion, you will feel the loss of your friend's physicality, the simple ability to hug your companion close in physical communion. Allow yourself to express this grief in the manner that feels natural to you, in the way that suits you. You may want to scream and cry or sit quietly for hours with your animal's favorite toys. You may want other people around you or you may want to be alone. You may want to take a break from grieving and laugh. Give yourself permission to experience whatever emotion is there for you in the moment. And give yourself permission to choose your rules of grief without judgment. This is not a test. There is no one qualified to grade your behavior. There is only what serves you.

Letting go of rules and expectations on how to grieve is an important way you can take care of yourself as you deal with the physical loss of your dear animal companion, and there are several other actions you can take in your journey of healing.

Give yourself permission to lean on your friends and family. Be honest with yourself about your needs and let yourself express these needs to those close to you. You may want to talk about your companion, you may want someone to sit quietly with you, or you may want time alone. Many of the people in your life will want to support and comfort you in your grief, and letting them know exactly what you need is a gift both to your loved ones and to yourself. It is possible that some of your friends and family will not understand how the loss of an animal can wound you so deeply. Give these people room to walk their own path as you walk yours. Their opinions and feelings about your grief are no more than that—opinions and feelings. Spend time with those who do understand and find compassion for those who do not.

If you are not the only one grieving the physical loss of your animal companion, reach out to these people or animals. You can best comfort another grieving soul by sharing your feelings with them, by leaning on them and letting them lean on you in return. Your courageous vulnerability will create a space in which they can be free to truly grieve and heal.

If you have other animal companions, you may find them to be an incredible source of comfort. Snuggle

145

with them, hug them, play with them, or talk with them about what you are feeling. And ask them about *their* grief. Animals grieve just as much as humans, and as they comfort you, you can also give comfort to them.

Writing about your animal companion, whether it be journaling, poems, or stories of your life together, can help you process the emotional tempest of your grief. If you choose to write about your animal companion, allow yourself to put your uncensored feelings into words. There are no right or wrong emotions when you are grieving, there are only the emotions this physical loss stirs in you. Give them room to be. If you are angry, let yourself be angry. If you are numb, allow yourself to be numb. Grief can be filled with emotions and thoughts that we label as bad or wrong. Give yourself room to feel and think whatever is there for you without judgment.

If you have a photo journal of your animal companion, you may want to spend time remembering the journey you and your animal shared. If you don't have a photo journal, you may find healing in creating one.

Grieving is a physical process as much as an emotional one. Take care of your body during this time by remembering to eat and rest. The grieving process can take a toll on your physical and mental stamina, draining your energy and leaving you in need of more rest than usual. Exercise can help support both your brain and your body as you grieve. Exercising, even in the form of a short walk, can increase chemicals in your brain related to enhanced moods and it can decrease stress hormones.

Give yourself as much time as you need to process this loss. Grieving is not a linear process. It is more like a capricious storm. The wind and rain of your emotions may blow with frightening force and then become calm only to swell again until the storm has run its course, always leaving the landscape of your soul marked by its passage.

If it has been weeks, months, or even years since your animal companion transitioned and you still break into tears at a sudden memory or thought, give yourself room to experience these emotions. It is not a weakness, but the natural expression of a corporeal soul missing the physical expression of another. The day will come when the memory of your animal companion's physical self will bring you more laughter than tears. Allow yourself to arrive at that day on your own schedule.

Chapter Ten Workbook Exercises

1. Give yourself permission to grieve—however long it takes, whatever form it takes.

2. Make a list of what your friends and family can do to support you during this time. Allow yourself to ask for this support.

3. Look up pet loss support groups in your area. Attend a meeting if this resonates with you and talk freely about the feeling the physical loss of your animal companion stirs in you.

4. Give yourself permission to grieve—however long it takes, whatever form it takes.

CHAPTER ELEVEN

Along the Path

Cruz

It's a beautiful fall day and the backyard is dotted with crisp yellow leaves. The chilly wind delivers more leaves from the branches above to join their companions on the ground where they briefly swirl in an autumn dance of change and continuity. I'm watching Capo, our four-year-old, chase the crunchy leaves with her two puppies, Jenks and Pink. They are energized by the cooler weather and they run circles around each other and me, their eyes bright with joy as they play.

My sweet thirteen-year-old boy Cruz is with us too, hunting for fallen apples under the apple tree. He is staying away from the rambunctious play of the other dogs. He has long since lost the ability and the desire to play a game of chase. He prefers a quiet and short stroll followed by treats and a nap. His legs are not as steady as they once were and they sometimes give out underneath him. His ears hear only the highest pitched sounds and his eyes see less of the world than they did a few years ago.

Now and again, he interrupts his apple hunting to look up and meet my eyes, checking in with me. Each time, he mentally tells me he is still content, still happy, that he still wants to be in this Cruz body . . . for now.

As I watch him totter around the apple tree, I realize I'm holding my breath. We are just on the edge, Cruz and I. I'm afraid to see him too clearly, and I'm afraid not to.

We are several months in to Cruz's treatment for Cushing's Disease. While he is doing much better, we are still playing a delicate balancing game. His body is adjusting to the medication and we go regularly for blood work to make sure he is still on the correct dosage. Not enough and his symptoms will return, too much and we run the risk of developing Addison's Disease.

He wants this and I would do anything to keep him with me while he still wants to stay. The twice daily medicine, the regular checkups, and the constant monitoring are easy for me. They give me something concrete to do for my little boy.

The hard part is being willing to truly listen to him, truly see him. As we have gotten his Cushing's Disease under control, I've become aware of just how unsteady his legs are. I've become aware of how much he sleeps now and how rarely he wants to play. I am happy that he wants to stay and I do not want to see or hear anything that would tell me otherwise.

I should be facing his illness and old age with fearless and unhesitating honesty. After all, I've participated in many conscious transitions and I've even written this book about them! I should feel prepared and honored to facilitate Cruz's coming transition from this life to the next. Instead, I vacillate between that precious fearless honesty and the mental version of squeezing my eyes shut and covering my ears every time he snuggles close to tell me how he feels.

One day, maybe soon, he's going to tell me he's tired. He's going to tell me he's not having fun anymore and he has other adventures awaiting him outside of his age-worn body. And I will need to hear him. I will need to love him enough to help him transition. I will need to put aside my need to keep him with me, to see only what I want to see, so that I can help him.

I think we all vacillate as we near our animal companions' transitions. I think this is part of being human, of learning what we are here to learn. I don't think this is meant to be emotionally easy, I think it's meant to be a journey of growth and new understanding each time. Whether this is your first conscious transition or your ninety-first, you may find yourself struggling with what your animal is asking of you. And that's all right.

There are no levels to master in conscious transitions, no point at which you will have "arrived." Each one will be a new experience; each one will push your growth and understanding just a little farther and in new directions.

You can be completely aware and in communication with your animal friend and still resist his or her transition. There will still be messages you don't want to hear and signs you don't want to see. But when you choose to be conscious and aware as your animal companion transitions, you will not miss the important messages, you will not miss the important signs. You will gain the beauty of learning and growing with your cherished friend.

Allow this process to be whatever it is for you. It will be your vulnerability, your *authenticity* that will make your animal companion's conscious transition perfect. The only way to get it right is to let go of getting it right.

I don't know if I will get everything right as Cruz and I walk the path of his transition, but I do know that I am already learning from him, already growing from this experience. I do know I am honored that he chose to be in my life and honored that he trusts me to hear him and respect his wishes.

Your animal companion has chosen you. Your animal companion trusts you to hear the messages and see the signs when the time comes. Trust yourself as much as your animal does. You may cover your ears and squeeze your eyes shut today, but when you set a course for a conscious transition, you will find the awareness and courage you need waiting for you along the path.

AFTERWORD

Has your animal companion left their body, or are you dealing with the upcoming transition of your animal friend? If so, please know that this book is from my heart to yours. I don't pretend to fully understand the emotions this transition causes for you, but I do understand how this event can be both painful and beautiful. I do know how the transition of your beloved animal can leave you breathless with pain and also full of wonder and love.

When we truly open our hearts and souls to the animals in our lives, we begin a journey of learning with them. They can become our teachers, especially around the time of their transition. They teach us about love, and they teach us about acceptance. They teach us about being authentic. They show us what we think of as our best selves and our worst selves, and they ask us to accept it all without judgment. They ask us to live in the moment with them, even in the moment of their transition.

My Roxy often told me that humans spend too much time on the concept of finality. "There is no final," she told me, "only the next lesson, the next remembering, the next opportunity to live in love with all around you."

She told me this more often as her transition neared, and I came to understand she was teaching me to look past the ending of her current body and see that the soul known as Roxy and the soul known as Andrea would continue our journey together.

Roxy's words are for you, too. You and the soul that is your animal companion are on a journey together. You have chosen to be with each other at this time and in this place. Your animal companion's transition is only a part of your journey.

It is my intent, requested and drawn from the infinite universe, that this book will give you the tools to walk this part of your journey together with love and fearless understanding, with connection, comfort, and peace.

From my heart to yours, I send blessings for your journey.

RESOURCES

Argus Institute: http://csuvth.colostate.edu/diagnostic_and_support/argus/

The Human/Animal Bond Trust: http://www.humananimalbondtrust.org/

The Association of Pet Loss and Bereavement . . .
Understanding Euthanasia:
http://aplb.org/services/euthanasia.html

International Association of Animal Hospice and
Palliative Care: http://iaahpc.org/

ABOUT THE AUTHOR

Andrea Floyd's life has been shaped by animals. Her earliest friend was a German Shepherd Dog named Rex. Andrea and Rex spent long hours in conversation and companionship. She considers Rex, and all the other animals in her childhood as her most important teachers.

Andrea is a professional Animal Communicator and freelance writer who writes most often about the human relationship with animals.

Andrea currently lives in Colorado with her husband, Jordan and their three dogs, Capo, Jenks and Pink, and their cat, Tux.

For more information, or to contact Andrea, visit *AndrealFloyd.com.*

Made in the USA
Charleston, SC
24 June 2013